"Therapists must have a deep understanding of the self—how it develops, how it can trap us, and how to change self-concepts. Our self shapes everything: our thoughts, emotions, behaviors, relationships, and careers. In this important book, Beate Ebert dives into theory and practice, producing an essential resource for therapist training and supervision. Study this book and you'll gain greater insight into yourself as a therapist, support your clients in recognizing the traps of their past, and help them move toward the lives they hope to live."

—**Louise Hayes, PhD**, clinical psychologist and adjunct senior research fellow at La Trobe University, developer of DNA-V, and coauthor of *What Makes You Stronger* and *Your Life Your Way*

"Beate Ebert beautifully integrates theory, metaphor, and lived experience to illuminate how to make self-as-context tangible in session. Chapter seven is especially powerful—it centers the therapeutic relationship as the most important intervention we have. This book is a must-read for clinicians committed to integrating presence, perspective taking, and compassion into their practice. It will shift how you show up with clients—and perhaps, how you show up with yourself."

—**Mavis Tsai, PhD**, research scientist at the University of Washington; cocreator of functional analytic psychotherapy; and founder of the Awareness, Courage & Love Global Project

"This is the book on self-as-context we've been waiting for! Beate Ebert brings rare clarity and compassion to one of ACT's most elusive processes. With humility and wisdom, she shows how perspective taking is not a concept to grasp but a presence to embody. A moving, practical, and essential guide for any therapist aiming to reach the heart of human suffering and healing."

—**Louise McHugh, PhD**, professor of psychology at University College Dublin, peer-reviewed ACT trainer, fellow of the Association for Contextual Behavioral Science (ACBS), and coauthor of *A Contextual Behavioral Guide to the Self*

"Self-as-context is a central theoretical component of acceptance and commitment therapy (ACT). Beate Ebert has produced a brilliant text that brings psychology, metaphysics, and spirituality into your clinical practice. This book will make you a better clinician, and might also help you understand yourself. I highly recommend it."

—**Stefan G. Hofmann, PhD**, Alexander von Humboldt Professor at Philipps University of Marburg, and coauthor of *Learning Process-Based Therapy*

"Of all the concepts in ACT, self-as-context is perhaps the most difficult to grasp. Beate Ebert has succeeded in writing a text that both explores this process theoretically and gives practical direction on how to use it in psychotherapy. Well done!"

—**Niklas Törneke, MD**, psychiatrist, licensed psychotherapist, and author of *Using Functional Analysis in Psychotherapy*

"When learning ACT, almost all practitioners struggle to understand the concept of self-as-context—and even more so, to apply it in useful therapeutic interventions. The good news is, in this well-written textbook, Beate Ebert takes you step by step through both the theory and clinical application of self-as-context, and the myriad ways you can use it to help both yourself and your clients live richer, fuller lives. I believe this to be the clearest and most practical text ever written on the topic of self-as-context. Highly recommended for all ACT practitioners of all levels—beginner, intermediate, or advanced."

—**Russ Harris, MBBS**, author of *ACT Made Simple* and *The Happiness Trap*

"*Self-as-Context in Therapy* fills a crucial gap in the ACT literature. By seamlessly weaving together real-life stories with core theoretical concepts, Dr. Ebert provides an elegant and effortless pathway to greater well-being for our clients and ourselves. I learned a lot from reading this book—and you will too."

—**Jennifer Kemp, MPsych**, author of *The ACT Workbook for Perfectionism*, and coauthor of *The Neurodivergence Skills Workbook for Autism and ADHD*

"One of the least understood yet most important ACT processes has finally been elucidated, both conceptually and as an innovative set of interventions, in *Self-as-Context in Therapy*. In Beate Ebert's new book, ACT therapists now have a clear road map to help clients enter and maintain awareness as the observer self."

—**Matthew McKay, PhD**, coauthor of *Acceptance and Commitment Therapy for Interpersonal Problems* and *Acceptance and Commitment Therapy for Couples*

"Self-as-context remains one of ACT's most challenging yet essential processes. This book brilliantly transforms a complex psychological concept into accessible, practical guidance. Dr. Ebert integrates developmental theory, relational frame theory (RFT), and moving clinical stories to show how self-as-context supports every other ACT process. She extends applications from individual therapy to couples, groups, and societal issues—providing comprehensive clinical guidance with concrete interventions that transform abstract concepts into practical tools."

—**Jenna LeJeune, PhD**, psychologist; president of Portland Psychotherapy Clinic, Research, and Training Center; and coauthor of *Values in Therapy*

"Self-as-context is a process and skill that serves both enlightenment and gaining freedom from the old agendas that often arise from hurtful events we did not choose to experience. Following these old agendas, with their rules and triggers, is, therefore, a kind of alien control. In her masterful book, Dr. Ebert shows how we can dampen or even overcome this alien determination and gain more self-control and self-determination of our lives."

—**Rainer F. Sonntag, MD**, behavioral psychiatrist and psychotherapist

"What makes this book especially valuable is its clinical practicality. Through examples, metaphors, and exercises, Dr. Ebert illustrates how therapists can notice and support the small but powerful moments where clients realize they're the observers of their experiences, not defined by them. She demonstrates how these shifts emerge through relationships, not just reasoning alone."

—**Joseph Ciarrochi, PhD**, professor of psychology at Australian Catholic University, developer of DNA-V, and coauthor of *What Makes You Stronger* and *The Thriving Adolescent*

Self-as-Context in Therapy

Help Your Clients Build a Flexible Self with Acceptance & Commitment Therapy

Beate M.E. Ebert

CONTEXT PRESS
An Imprint of New Harbinger Publications, Inc.

Publisher's Note

This publication is designed to provide accurate and authoritative information in regard to the subject matter covered. It is sold with the understanding that the publisher is not engaged in rendering psychological, financial, legal, or other professional services. If expert assistance or counseling is needed, the services of a competent professional should be sought.

NEW HARBINGER PUBLICATIONS is a registered trademark of New Harbinger Publications, Inc.

New Harbinger Publications is an employee-owned company.

New Harbinger Publications, Inc.
5674 Shattuck Avenue
Oakland, CA 94609
www.newharbinger.com

Grateful acknowledgment is made to the clients who have given permission to print their quotes in this work.

Cover design by Amy Daniel

Acquired by Elizabeth Hollis Hansen

Edited by M. C. Calvi

Library of Congress Cataloging-in-Publication Data on file

FSC
www.fsc.org
MIX
Paper | Supporting responsible forestry
FSC® C008955

Printed in the United States of America

27 26 25

10 9 8 7 6 5 4 3 2 1 First Printing

This book is dedicated to my loving Dad.

Contents

FOREWORD

A Process to be Practiced

"Self-as-context" is not exactly a phrase that rolls off the tongue—or, for that matter, one that readily calls up a rich human experience. And yet, of all the processes in the ACT model, none points more directly to the mystery and possibility of being human than this difficult-to-name process.

You can talk about it in technical terms—as a perspective-taking repertoire, as the locus of consciousness, as a function of relational framing—but none of those quite touch the core of it. How do we help a person feel what it's like to be the one who notices their experience—without inadvertently saying things that land outside of that healing experience? What do we say and what do we do, when a client is so entangled in a rigid self-story that they can't even imagine a sense of self that doesn't have edges—all the while knowing this very sense is the psychological foundation of their every conscious moment?

The book in your hands shines exactly there.

Beate has done something in this book that few ACT authors have done so skillfully: she has taken a subtle and seemingly abstract concept and grounded it in life as it is lived; in therapy as it is conducted. She does not teach self-as-context as a "topic" to be mastered; she teaches it as a process to be practiced. Moment by moment. With humility and patience. With clients who may be depressed, neurodivergent, grieving, in chronic pain—or, not uncommonly, in the room and yet unreachable, because something essential has gone missing from their experience of themselves as they experience their own experience.

What went wrong? We see there are a myriad of pathways. The absence of emotional support in childhood. The legacy of trauma, or the corrosive effect of social comparison. The understandable retreat into avoidance and coherence-seeking that we all do when life gets too painful. But always, underneath these patterns, there's a yearning—for belonging, for clarity, for vitality, for meaning—and Beate keeps that yearning in full view.

Beate draws on the psychological flexibility model as we've known it but she adds needed nuance: mapping each core ACT process to the deep human need it serves. In her hands, self-as-context becomes a return to something original and intimate: the sense that we are not just the stories we carry, not just the pain we've endured, but the one who has been there all along, witnessing, noticing, appreciating, living.

Beate brings to this work the sensibility of both a seasoned therapist and a deeply thoughtful human being. She weaves research, personal stories, metaphor, and case examples into a rich narrative that is easy to follow without being simplistic. She tells the truth about what it's like when therapy falters—noticing when her interventions land flat because the client is not yet able to reflect on their experience or take a broader view of themselves. And she gives the reader tools to do better:

moment-to-moment exercises, therapeutic language, and conceptual clarity that supports both client and therapist in making contact with the deepest sense of self.

I was touched by the personal story Beate shares of her father—a quiet teacher of self-as-context long before there was a name for it. There is something profound in the simple and direct way she describes his open presence, his capacity to relate to people and animals and trees as if they were all part of the same unqualified whole. It gives texture to the idea that the observing self is ally of compassion, inclusion, and connection. It's a kind of invisible dome under which life can prosper.

You'll find all of that in this book. And you'll find more: a developmental perspective on the emergence of self, grounded in Relational Frame Theory; a framework for working with inflexible self-content that doesn't pathologize the client's history; and a constant reminder that the goal of therapy isn't to erase pain, but to open space for action and meaning, even in its presence.

What Beate has offered here is a deeply human book. It's scientifically informed and clinically astute, but it's also personal, humble, and refreshingly honest. She never overclaims. She simply invites us to walk alongside her—and alongside our clients—as fellow travelers learning to see ourselves more clearly, hold our experiences more lightly, and choose a life that reflects what we truly care about.

If you're a therapist who has struggled to bring this deeper sense of self into the room, or if you've wondered how to help clients who seem locked in their self-narratives, this book is for you. If you're looking for a guide to flexibility processes that respects both the science and the soul of ACT, this book is for you. And if, like me, you believe that the purpose of therapy is not just to reduce suffering, but to help people become more whole, connected, and free—then I think you'll find a trusted companion in these pages.

Beate Ebert has written a beautiful and practical book. I'm glad it's in the world.

—Steven C. Hayes, Ph.D
Foundation Professor Emeritus, University of Nevada, Reno
Originator and co-Developer of Acceptance and Commitment Therapy

INTRODUCTION

Welcome to the Journey

Welcome to our shared journey of building a more flexible self. This book is written for therapists, but hopefully in a way that is useful for anyone interested in a flexible self. Since we all live with our own selves, the topic touches each of us. The way we relate to ourselves can be kind and nurturing, or painful and invalidating. We all yearn to be valued and loved. Through practice, we can learn to look at ourselves with kindness, accept what we see, and embrace the awareness that we are much more than our own self-perception.

As a therapist, you hopefully have many clients with whom you feel comfortable—where nothing seems to go wrong, therapy unfolds naturally, you feel creative, and you experience yourself at your best.

Perhaps you also have clients with whom you feel tense, cautious, or like you are walking on eggshells. You may feel unsure about what to offer them, sensing that therapy is not progressing well. You might even wonder what you are actually working on with them, uncertain about the quality of your therapeutic relationship.

These feelings can be important indicators that self-as-context is a key process to explore. In the past, I sometimes unintentionally pressured clients with exercises that focused on agreed-upon goals, acceptance, or defusion—without recognizing that their capacity to recognize and name their own experiences, or to take a more distant perspective on themselves or others, was not yet well developed. The foundation was missing, and as a result, the interventions did not yield meaningful results.

Your clients may face challenges such as insomnia, self-criticism, social anxiety, grief, depression, chronic pain, neurodivergence, watching a loved one struggle, or coping with declining health. Often, they will become consumed by their internal experiences, unable to see a clear path forward.

You can help by guiding them toward greater presence—encouraging them to step back and view their grief and struggles from a broader perspective, integrating all their experiences as part of themselves. From there, they may begin to see a wider range of meaningful actions available to them. This is the essence of self-as-context.

For you as a therapist, learning about self-as-context can open up new ideas for interventions. You may discover that small adjustments lead to refreshing, easier, and more effective ways to move forward—often bringing about a new quality of life for your clients.

My hope is that this book will lighten your burden as a clinician and serve as a resource for your own well-being. When you struggle with self-as-context, please remember: it is a process. Every step along the way is valuable, and you can always continue practicing it for yourself and your clients.

What I Learned from My Dad

I had a wonderful teacher for self-as-context, even though he had never heard of the concept. My dad was a deeply loving man, a hardworking mechanic, and well known in our village for helping anyone in need. If a farmer showed up early on a Sunday morning with a broken tractor, desperate to bring in the harvest, my father would put on his work overalls, grab his toolbox, and go fix it—no questions asked.

We often went hiking in the woods, and whenever we met someone, my dad would start a conversation. I remember asking him, "Dad, do you know this person?" and he would simply smile and say, "Now I do." He didn't just talk to people—he spoke to dogs and cats that crossed his path, sometimes even to trees.

What does this have to do with self-as-context? My dad was a master at creating a safe and inclusive space—not only for me, but for everyone around him. He related to people, animals, and plants as if they were a natural extension of himself.

I only fully understood the power of his loving presence when he passed away years ago. It felt as if the air had changed, as if an invisible protective cover had suddenly disappeared. It took me a year and a half to rebuild that space for myself. That process was about developing trust in myself and in what truly matters to me, without letting desperate feelings or discouraging thoughts take over. In other words, I had to practice self-as-context.

I am deeply grateful that I learned this ability early on through my father. I have no doubt that his presence shaped my ability to find supportive, loving mentors, supervisors, and coaches—without whom I wouldn't be writing this book.

Regardless of whether life has offered us the ideal conditions in which to develop a flexible self, or significant challenges, every experience can contribute to our growth when integrated with awareness. This process takes practice, but it is deeply rewarding. As we expand our capacity for relating to ourselves with clarity, soberness, and kindness, we become more present, more fulfilled—and often, we start noticing opportunities that were invisible to us before.

Perception Is Key

This book is about expanding perspectives, increasing choices, and cultivating flexibility and awareness.

Perception is key—it is our gateway to the world. It shapes how we connect to everything, both within and beyond ourselves. The broader and clearer our perception, the more possibilities we can see. The more viewpoints we consider, the richer our awareness becomes.

Self-as-context offers the most comprehensive perspective we can take. It encompasses all our experiences, including those that are preverbal, nonverbal, and beyond words. Each of us holds a unique view of the world—we could say that with every person, a world arises and disappears. From self-as-context, we gain the widest range of possible actions—far greater than when operating from our habitual, everyday self that simply wakes up and thinks, "Here I am again."

The perspective of self-as-context is accessible from any therapeutic approach. Please bring in all your expertise as a clinician and adapt the proposed exercises to suit your clients and their needs. However, simply acquiring knowledge is not enough. To apply self-as-context effectively, you must explore it for yourself. It is an adventurous journey, and I hope this book serves as a valuable guide and companion along the way.

Self-as-Context in Therapy is written from a functional contextualist perspective—one of many possible worldviews. Politics, philosophy, psychology, physics, spirituality—each offers its own lens through which we can understand the world. These perspectives are all valid, contributing to the diversity we have developed as humans, yet none holds all of the truth.

I chose the framework of contextual behavioral science (CBS), rooted in the philosophy of functional contextualism (FC), because it underpins my therapeutic approach, acceptance and commitment therapy (ACT). CBS provides a science-based perspective on the self, aiming not only to understand, but also to predict and influence behavior. It is a pragmatic worldview that supports my goal of effective clinical intervention.

We all stand on the shoulders of elders who came before us, in our own fields and beyond. While this book does not delve deeply into the vast history of self-research, we are looking back on millennia of human inquiry on the question, "Who am I?"

This book is also written from my personal perspective: a sixty-one-year-old German psychologist, female, neurodiverse like all of us in some way, yet fairly neurotypical, drawing from twenty-five years as a practitioner, eighteen years of ACT training, and a decade as a peer-reviewed ACT trainer.

I appreciate your trust.

Now, let's begin the journey.

CHAPTER 1

How the Self Develops

We all move through life accompanied by our own sense of self, often giving little thought to how this self came into being. We believe it is just who we are, as it is what we have always known. However, the self develops in fascinating ways, and understanding this process provides valuable points of intervention for psychotherapeutic work.

Behavior can only be understood in its context: if you want to understand why somebody is running, it's essential to know whether they're doing so for exercise, because somebody is following them at night, or because they simply can't wait to hug their child.

For this reason, we must look at self-development as a response to a person's context.

In early life, that context could be a caregiver smiling at their baby, with the baby smiling back—no words required. Or the context could also be internal, like a pain in the abdomen, making the baby cry as a response to its inner experience. As soon as language is involved, however, context and responding become much more complex.

In acceptance and commitment therapy (ACT), we draw from a functional contextual theory on language called relational frame theory (RFT). This theory explains how language and cognition are acquired through interactions with the environment. It will help us to see how language allows us to build a self, why we can get stuck in our self-knowledge, and how different aspects of the self can help us to get unstuck again.

In RFT, the self is seen as a verbal repertoire, involving not only our psychological content—thoughts, feelings, bodily sensations, and actions—but also the verbal awareness of this content and verbal responses to it (Stewart & McHugh, 2012).

For example, the thought "I am hungry" when you notice your grumbling stomach is a part of your self, as is the mental image of the food you crave and your choice to eat. Maybe you are heading straight to the snack bar to get the biggest burger, and you know yourself like that. How you say hello to the person at the snack bar is also part of your self, along with the way it feels when you eat the food. You might recognize your deep satisfaction after eating, thinking, "Wow, this is simply the best burger in town," and also notice a familiar thought in the background: "Darn, I actually wanted to live healthier." There's also the part of your self that notices everything you're doing, thinking, and feeling, including your digestion in action. Parts of your digestion are not verbally accessible, but the result—your digestion working well or not—is definitely part of your self-experience. Hopefully this gives you an idea of what makes up your self. But let's start at the very beginning.

1.1 Natural-Born Social Beings

Babies are born entirely dependent on others for nourishment, care, and comfort. They have no problem tormenting their parents with loud cries in the middle of the night—which typically elicits immediate soothing. Babies don't worry that their parents might become frustrated or love them less; they would need language to have thoughts like that.

Before they learn the meaning of words, babies have no explicit sense of self. Instead, they have a preverbal awareness of their own experiences—such as tension, relaxation, and feelings of comfort or discomfort—and they express those sensations accordingly. Babies actively seek interactions and even initiate them. Remarkably, newborns can recognize, remember, and imitate facial expressions (Beebe, Cohen, & Lachmann, 2019). From their earliest moments, they begin to notice relationships between events, such as between their own bodily feelings and their caregivers' reactions. For example, when a baby is upset, the caregiver might recognize that feeling and mirror it in an empathic way, thereby fostering a safe relationship. Recognizing and mirroring the baby's expressions—often intuitively in an exaggerated manner—typically leads to successful soothing. In contrast, unresponsive, defensive, or even harsh reactions can heighten the baby's distress and increase their cries for comfort (Beebe et al., 2019).

For healthy self-development, babies need a safe, nurturing environment—both physically and emotionally. This environment is created by caregivers who engage in gentle physical and verbal contact, and show genuine interest in the baby's facial expressions and preverbal signals. To develop a mind and a conscious sense of self, a baby ideally needs the consistent presence and connection of others. The behavior of caregivers significantly shapes the developing brain's wiring. As psychologist Lisa Feldman Barrett puts it, "it takes more than one brain to create a mind" (2017, p. 153).

Babies also begin to form early expectations about what will happen next. For example, when a baby opens their mouth and the mother reliably responds with a smile, the baby will start to anticipate the mother's reaction. When predictions are successful, babies experience a sense of efficacy, making it naturally reinforcing. Throughout the day, the baby is constantly filtering countless impressions, sorting out which ones are important or connected. For instance, the baby may notice that a particular ringing sound is often followed by the mother talking to someone. After learning language, the kid will call this "a phone call," but the components of the event have already been wired by multiple learning experiences much earlier (Feldman Barrett, 2017).

1.2 Language: Our Human Superpower

Self-awareness explodes to unprecedented complexity when children learn language.

Newborns are especially attuned to human language and can distinguish it from any surrounding noise. They pay even closer attention when adults use "baby talk"—speaking in a higher pitch, using short sentences, and making eye contact—and nearly all parents are "intuitive teachers" (Novak, 2012, p. 77; Feldman Barrett, 2017). Parents provide the context for children to relate words to things, for example by naming an object the child is grabbing, saying, "Yeah, your little froggy," or by holding up a thing, like an apple, and naming it.

This "naming game" (Novak, 2012, p. 87) is fostering joint attention and social interaction between the child and the parent, seen as precursors to building a self.

At first it is just a repetition, but little by little, toddlers find meaning in words. They are learning frequently repeated words and associating those words with the context in which they occur. For instance, after many experiences, the baby learns that the sound "mom" appears together with the presence of a familiar person, her scent, her touch, and the feeling of comfort (Feldman Barrett, 2017).

It is a complex learning step to go from just repeating words to learning that the person "mom" is equal to the word "mom." It is called "bidirectional learning" in RFT. So, when dad says the word "mom," the child will look for mom, even when mom is not present in the room.

In this way, children learn that words refer to objects—and eventually learn that the word is the object itself, which, of course, it is not. The word "dog" is not the actual dog, but teaching it that way would be far too complicated, such as: "This animal with four legs and a tail is called 'dog' in the English-speaking community." Instead, they simply learn: "This is a dog," "This is a chair," "This is a tree," and so on.

They understand that each object in their world is "the same as" a word and that there is a "right" word for every thing. Everyone is pleased when they use the right word, which is very motivating. The relation of "same as/different from" is often the first type of relational frame children learn. Over time, they also learn many others, like "smaller than/bigger than," "better/worse," "more/less," and "part of." These ways of relating things to one another help children make sense of the world. Step by step, children become part of the language community, and the use of this new skill is also reinforced internally, as it feels good to participate in a common "truth."

The complexity of human language—and they fact that children can learn it so rapidly—is possible because a child does not need to learn everything through direct experience. Simply by hearing others, they can draw conclusions—for example, that previously insignificant ants are actually dangerous creatures that bite. I conducted this early psychological experiment as a child with my younger brother, vividly describing how ants can bite. Although no ant had actually bitten him, the "experiment" ended with my father carrying him all the way back through the forest, because my brother refused to touch the ground again.

My brother did not just establish a connection between "biting ants," and "dangerous to touch the ground"—which is known in RFT terms as "derived relational responding." There was also a "transformation of stimulus function": the previously neutral ant (stimulus function: "harmless") became a threatening object (stimulus function: "dangerous")—purely through language, without direct experience.

These verbal abilities appear to be unique to the human species. However, as this example shows, they can lead to unhelpful assumptions—not only about ants, but also for instance about our self-image.

Yet, acquiring language initially seems like gaining a superpower. A whole new world opens up. The baby learns to say "mom," and Mom lights up with joy. The baby points at something and says "dog," and Dad proudly confirms, "Yes, that's our dog, Buddy." The baby names its toy "teddy bear," and Grandpa will hand it over with a smile. It is a complex learning process, and the baby becomes a little magician, using words to make things happen.

1.3 What's Happening Inside Me?

This learning process also applies to the inner world. Every internal experience—every emotion, every bodily sensation—has a name that children can learn with the help of their caregivers.

It's a significant move from simply feeling a sensation to knowing what that feeling is. For example, the feeling of hunger is present from the beginning. However, recognizing that the sensation in the stomach is called "hunger"—and understanding that it is "I" who feels hunger—is a major developmental step (McHugh, Stewart, & Almada, 2019).

As we've seen, naming objects gives us access to them. The same is true for inner experiences. When a toddler learns the word "hungry," they can use it to express that they want to eat, as the word itself implies the solution to the problem. Even before learning language, a baby already has a concept of hunger, formed from repeated experiences of bodily discomfort and the caregiver's responses to the child's nonverbal cues (Feldman Barrett, 2017). However, understanding and using the word "hungry" provides a much more precise tool to express the need—and ideally, to receive immediate relief in the form of food.

Recognizing and naming our internal experiences is a powerful way to better understand ourselves and to communicate our wants and needs. We can learn language only with others, which is even more true for naming inner experiences. While you can point to a thing or a person, you can't point to a feeling—you need somebody else to tell you the word "hunger" and relate it to the specific sensation in your body. Parents do this naturally, often, and in various situations by saying things like, "Oh dear, you're crying—are you hungry? Let's get some food." Over time, the child starts to associate the word "hunger" with the bodily experience and the solution of eating.

Parents also show interest in their child's preferences and internal experiences through questions and observations, such as "Are you tired?" "I think you like this strawberry ice cream," or "Should we cuddle?" These cues foster the child's curiosity about their own feelings and needs (Skinner, 1976). By listening and receiving feedback, children learn to name what they notice, giving them a more conscious access to their internal world.

1.4 Becoming Oneself

A critical advancement for a child in developing a sense of self is finally recognizing that their own person is distinct from others, and that their own behavior is distinct from others' behavior (McHugh, & Stapleton, 2021).

Initially, toddlers use simple phrases like, "Joey tired," "Mummy angry." When asked about breakfast, they might even mention what their sibling ate instead of their own meal. At this stage, a toddler has not yet developed a clear concept of themself as a person with continuous internal experiences that stretch from the past into the future (Stewart & McHugh, 2012).

But as they learn language, children observe others and listen to others in various situations, and parents often say things like "You are my little girl," "I am hungry. Are you hungry too?" and "I love how you smile at daddy, sweetheart."

Gradually children learn so-called "deictic" relations —relational frames that are "particularly abstract" (McHugh et al., 2019, p. 83) and organized around the speaker's perspective. For example, "here" only makes sense in contrast to "there," "now" refers to a different point in time than "then" and "you" only exists in relation to "I" (Stewart & McHugh, 2012).

These relations are not easy for a child to grasp, for example to understand that they are "here" and their playmate is "there," yet, when they walk over to their playmate's spot and stand there, they are still "here" from their own perspective, not "there."

In everyday interactions, children are frequently asked questions involving these relational concepts, such as "What are you seeing now?" "What is your brother doing there?" "Where did you go yesterday?" "What will we do tomorrow?" Over time, in finding the correct responses to these exchanges, children build an awareness of their own distinct point of view.

Eventually, children do not only grasp the meaning of "here" and "there," and understand that events can occur now, in the past, or in the future—what they come to call "then." They do not only understand that they are separate from "mom," "dad," and anyone else. As they gain these relational skills, they also implicitly learn that they have a consistent perspective—that they perceive everything from their "I," which is always here and now (McHugh et al., 2019). As children develop the ability to take perspectives about themselves, they also begin to understand that others have their own consistent perspectives.

This process is known as "perspective-taking," where children gradually come to experience a consistent sense of self ("I") that extends through time. However, they also implicitly learn that self-awareness can only occur in the present moment—now. Moreover, while their physical location can change, their sense of "I" is always right "here." This crucial developmental milestone typically emerges around the age of four (Stewart & McHugh, 2012).

Subsequently, in various social situations, children also recognize how their behaviors and feelings influence those of others, as in "Oh, I was jumping in the puddle with my new clothes, and mom doesn't look happy at all." The social self develops progressively. McHugh, Stewart, and Almada (2019, p. 77) state, "When the social environment is rich and an individual is developing typically, awareness of the self and awareness of others develop in tandem."

Once children realize that others are distinct beings, what others think about them becomes important. Before acquiring language, they were social beings who naturally belonged. Now, however, they are beings who want to belong. They start applying the relational concepts they learned earlier, like "same as" (e.g., the word "dog" is the same as the animal dog), "different from" (e.g., a cat is different from a dog), and "more than/less than," and "part of" to themselves: "I'm a sportsperson," "I'm not as tall as Maggie," "I'm smarter than John," "I wasn't chosen to be part of this team."

This marks the point where the content of the self becomes important, when children begin to assess and compare their body and abilities to those of others ("I am less attractive than my friend," "I don't have a dad like everybody else."), or to judge feelings, thoughts, and behaviors as right or wrong, which leads to self-content (e.g., "I am not attractive," "Something is wrong with me.").

To some extent, assessing and comparing themselves to others leads children to adjust, so they belong, which is part of our social nature; it is a prerequisite to build a common culture and get along with each other

The downside is that children sometimes conform so much in order to belong that they lose the ability to develop in a healthy way. This is especially true when they grow up in unfavorable circumstances, with caregivers who fail to provide the rich, supportive, and reliable feedback that children need. Unhealthy behavioral patterns can emerge and persist into adulthood. A child may stop paying attention to their own inner experiences because those experiences don't align with parental expectations or because peers react negatively to their expressions.

1.5 How Does Building a Self Work Now?

Two main processes are essential for children to develop a sense of self:

1. Recognizing and naming one's own experiences

This involves moving beyond simply experiencing events to knowing and describing what one feels, hears, sees, and does. In other words, developing the capacity to reflect on one's experiences and talk about them. In scientific terms, this process is called "tacting" (McHugh et al., 2019).

2. Learning about perspective-taking
Perspective-taking involves understanding that one's experiences always come from "I"—a perspective that is always "here" and "now." A person has no other vantage point. It also means recognizing that others—such as mom, dad, and other people—have their own perspectives, their own "I," along with their own unique wishes, feelings, and preferences. The relationships I-you, here-there, and now-then are abstract concepts that are only accessible through language. In scientific terms, these are referred to as "deictic relations" (McHugh et al., 2019).

These capacities allow the self to fill with content, enabling children to start constructing their own stories about themselves. These narratives become increasingly complex, as they include not only actual events from the children's lives, but also inferences about themselves from what they see happening to others. For example, seeing a teacher praise another child might lead to thoughts like, "I'm not that smart; otherwise, I would be praised too." Similarly, exposure to movies and social media can shape beliefs like "This is how I should look" or "This is how a boy should behave."

While these processes can be helpful for learning how to integrate into social group or avoid mistakes, they can also lead to rigid self-concepts. The self tends to be coherent, as coherence itself is highly reinforcing. It feels uncomfortable when something doesn't fit, so a child is more likely to notice information that aligns with their self-picture while overlooking details that don't. This tendency is discussed further in chapter 4.

As children grow, they receive countless opportunities to generate self-content every day through feedback from parents, peers, teachers, and others. This feedback elicits reactions, generates new feedback, and collaboratively shapes identity. The process is not a one-way street from caregivers to children, but a shared dynamic.

A child will prioritize certain feedback over others, depending on factors like who gives it, whether it occurs publicly, the child's prior experiences, and their personality. Some feedback sticks, becoming part of their self-concept: "I am this kind of person." However, neither children nor adults can fully control what feedback they adopt or how it impacts them.

For instance, a praising statement like "You are really smart" can be tricky. The child connects "smart" to "I" ("same as smart"), which seems positive because it brings enjoyable attention—dad looks happy. But the child might now feel pressure to always be smart, become frustrated when they don't feel smart, or even hide their struggles so as not to disappoint others. Smart/not smart has now become part of their self-concept, along with comparisons like smarter/less smart than others.

Instead, sharing observations (e.g., "Wow, I love how you persisted with this; I bet it wasn't easy") or asking open-ended questions (e.g., "How did you figure that out?" or "How do you think this could help with the next problem?") can be more beneficial in the long run. This way, children learn not to rely on fixed labels ("being smart is good") but rather to relate to their experiences in a more flexible and adaptive way.

Positive or negative cycles can also emerge (Villatte, Villatte, & Hayes, 2015). For example, a girl who feels happy around her friends might expect to feel the same in the future. She might say to her friends, "I can't wait to see you tomorrow," which reinforces her friends' enjoyment of her company, creating a positive cycle. Conversely, if one of her friends hurt her feelings, she might withdraw, avoid eye contact, and reduce social interaction. Over time, she may avoid her friends altogether, leading them to assume she's no longer interested in the friendship. This could confirm her difficult experience and perpetuate a negative cycle.

Whatever happens, the self continuously fills with content, and the child—later the adolescent and then the adult—comes to believe that this content defines who they are. However, what matters most is not the content itself, but the relationship they create with it.

We can notice certain thoughts and emotions while still deciding for ourselves how we want to act. This is why we cultivate the capacity for self-as-context, defined as "the stable perspective from which all self-relevant processes can be seen, including both problematic self-labeling as well as helpful self-based values" (McHugh, & Stapleton, 2021, p. 254). This perspective allows us to see our self-content not as "the truth," but as one perspective among many. It allows us to say, "Oh, yes, this is what I think about myself, but I can also see it differently and choose to act according to my values."

Let's explore how this might manifest in an adult's life when the development of the self has progressed successfully.

1.6 How Can We Imagine a Flexible Adult Person?

Building the self is an ongoing, lifelong process. At every stage of life—starting a new school, falling in love, losing a relationship, beginning a career, becoming a parent, facing illness, growing older, or encountering unexpected challenges—we encounter new limits to our flexibility and opportunities for learning. Yet, regardless of age, it is always possible to cultivate a more flexible sense of self.

In RFT terms, this involves continuously practicing the ability to recognize, label, and take perspective on one's experiences—observing them with distance while maintaining a low level of fusion or entanglement with one's self-content.

How this looks in clinical experience will be different for everyone, depending on context, culture, age, and personal circumstances. However, universally, a flexible person stays in good contact with their own perceptions and remains present for what is happening in the moment. Such a person can adapt their actions to meet the demands of a situation while accepting what lies beyond their control. They have a clear sense of their long-term values and align their actions accordingly, taking advantage of good opportunities. When immediate urges or automatic behaviors conflict with their commitments, they can recognize this conflict, reflect on what matters, and choose actions that align with their deeper intentions.

A flexible person is stable but not rigid. They make choices that feel satisfying and authentic, express themselves openly, and welcome the full range of internal experiences and emotions. They strive to understand the messages behind these emotions and act in ways that align with their goals and values.

These qualities also extend to relationships. A flexible person cultivates open and balanced connections, discerning which relationships are nurturing and which may be unhelpful or harmful. They can adapt to changes in relationships, collaborating effectively with individuals who share similar goals and values, while stepping away from draining or harmful interactions.

They build trust in themself and others, acknowledging both strengths and vulnerabilities. They aim to show kindness, generosity, and compassion toward themself and others, especially during challenging times. A flexible person maintains a healthy balance between their autonomy and their desire for connection. When feeling upset or stuck, they reconnect with themself, seek support, and find new perspectives or actions aligned with their values.

This description is not meant to define an ideal, but to encourage practicing these skills over time. The goal is not perfection, but to gradually gain easier and more frequent access to these capacities.

Expanding the self can be exciting, challenging, scary, or even enchanting. At times, it may also be painful—especially when life circumstances beyond our control force us to grow. However, everyone has the capacity to further develop their sense of self, and as therapists, we can support our clients in this process, regardless of the circumstances.

1.7 Summary

Self in ACT: The self is our ongoing, verbally based experience of events both within and outside of our bodies. This includes thoughts, feelings, bodily sensations, and visible actions, along with our continuous responses to these experiences through language.

The ideal foundation for a flexible self: Babies thrive in physically and emotionally safe environments, where caregivers provide reliable communication and connection. Through mirroring the child's expressions and offering multiple cues, caregivers help children learn about thoughts, feelings, bodily sensations, and actions.

What children need to develop their self:

1. To recognize and use language to accurately name their experiences in both their external and internal worlds.
2. To understand that their perspective—including their thoughts, feelings, bodily sensations, and behaviors—is unique and different from the perspectives of others. They must also grasp that their experience always comes from their own I, which exists only in the here and now.

> Lack of perspective led me to therapy in my late twenties. At times, I felt like I was no longer myself, completely lost in grief. Suddenly viewing my situation from "above" and with objectivity helped me put things into perspective, and this approach still supports me in difficult moments today.
>
> —Johanna, thirty-six years old, senior executive and mother

CHAPTER 2

Three Useful Aspects of the Self

To better understand the three aspects of the self described in this chapter, imagine a garden.

There's the ongoing growth of plants and movement of animals—like bees, butterflies, and snails. And there is us, the gardener, digging, planting, watering. This represents the ongoing experience of the self: our awareness as things happen, one moment after another. It's what we here refer to as self-as-process.

Then there's the content of the garden—flowers and vegetables we like, and the weeds we could do without. There are the bees that help the garden blossom and the snails eating our lettuce. This stands for the content of the self: thoughts, emotions, bodily sensations, roles, memories, and judgments—all the things we perceive and have opinions about. Because it's focused on the content, this is what we call it: self-as-content.

Finally, there's the part where we pause for a moment and look at the garden. We notice what's growing and thriving, or what's withering or missing. Maybe we are proud, or maybe we see room for improvement. We might become aware of our thoughts and hopes about the garden—without needing to act on them. This is self-as-context: the part of us that's aware of the ongoing flow and content, without being defined or changed by them.

The three aspects of the self provide a valuable framework for understanding the self and have proven highly effective in promoting clinical progress. From a developmental perspective, these aspects can be seen as "typically emerging" when a child is given appropriate training and support (McHugh et al., 2019, p. 5).

It is important to recognize that the scientific investigation and definition of these aspects remain a work in progress. Different sources may emphasize or prioritize certain elements differently. In the following pages, I will summarize the current state of research and application, focusing on what I see most relevant for us as therapists.

The development of the self relies on two key processes: (1) recognizing and naming one's own experiences, and (2) understanding that the "I" always experiences from a "here" and "now" perspective, while simultaneously recognizing that others have their own distinct viewpoints.

These capacities are considered prerequisites for the emergence of the three self-repertoires: self-as-process, self-as-content, and self-as-context (McHugh et al., 2019). Each aspect represents a unique way of experiencing the self and opens the door to various types of interventions:

- Self-as-process involves noticing and naming the ever-changing flow of experiences. This capacity helps clients stay grounded in the present moment and disrupts rigid patterns of behavior.
- Self-as-content, the narrative a person holds about themselves, is typically more static. While this can offer a sense of stability, it may also foster rigidity. Becoming aware of unhelpful self-content and creating distance from it can feel liberating.

- Self-as-context provides a perspective on both self-as-process and self-as-content. Engaging with this aspect can cultivate a more adaptive sense of stability and continuity. Unlike self-as-content, self-as-context remains consistent, yet it does so in a detached and flexible way.

These self-aspects are understood as behaviors, which is why the term "selfing" is sometimes used to describe them as actions. In this book, I will use the more common term "self" to refer to what we experience as the product of these actions. While each aspect has distinct properties, they are interconnected, with each relying on the others for effective functioning. By definition, these aspects can only develop through the use of language (McHugh et al., 2019).

2.1 Self-as-Process

Before language, a toddler has no concept or consciousness of the self; they are just alive and kicking, fully immersed in the ongoing, ever-changing flow of life. They are a part of this flow, as they would need language to see themself as separate from it. When they begin to acquire language, they start to distinguish the various events happening inside their body and around themself, changing over time. This marks the very early beginning of what we define as the self.

2.1.1 Developing Verbal Self-Awareness

In RFT terms, self-as-process is described as "the knowing self, or self as an ongoing process of verbal relations" (McHugh et al., 2019, p. 106). It is also referred to as the "experiential self," which Hayes et al. (2020) explain as "an ongoing process of verbal self-awareness." In simpler terms, self-as-process refers to a person's conscious perception—their ability to recognize and name what they are experiencing as "I" or "me" in the moment. This includes what they perceive inside and outside their body, as well as what they do (e.g., "I feel sad," "I am tired," "I am sweating," "I see the bus coming," "I am playing."). Recognizing and labeling these experiences is essential for forming a sense of self, including preferences, wishes, needs, and characteristics. Terms like "mindfulness" or "present moment awareness" are closely related to self-as-process and are often used interchangeably. However, employing the term self-as-process emphasizes a specific focus on the self and more clearly highlights the scientifically defined capacity.

While the process of experiencing is present from birth, it is only with language that a child begins to relate these experiences to "I" and "me," and respond to them purposefully (e.g., "I am feeling hungry," followed by getting something to eat). Acquiring language profoundly transforms a child's relationship with their own experiences, because it allows them to express themself more fully and be understood.

Ideally, children are exposed to a wide variety of cues (e.g., "Do you like this cake?" "Are you tired?" "You look excited"), which helps them develop a rich inner world and appreciate the diversity of the external world. Over time, children begin articulating their preferences ("I like red better than blue"), needs and wishes ("I want Dad to read me a story before bed"), and boundaries ("I don't want to go to kindergarten"). They learn to recognize the context of a situation and adjust their behavior accordingly (e.g., "I feel anxious in the dark; I will ask my sister to come with me"). Additionally, they also explore their own autonomy. It can be challenging for parents to strike the right balance between allowing children to explore and express themselves freely, and also providing guidance with appropriate limits.

Self-as-process is where the self begins to be "filled with content." A verbal network originates. It will eventually grow into what an adult person identifies as their "self." This self-development is shaped by the feedback children receive from important figures in their lives. For example, if sadness is met with responses like "Come on, don't be such a crybaby," children are more likely to suppress those feelings in the future and judge themselves for having those feelings. Conversely, if a parent says, "Come here, honey, let's be sad together," the child is more likely to feel safe expressing sadness again and accepting it as part of the emotional spectrum.

As children grow older and their worlds expand, more and more influencing factors come into play, such as cultural norms, social communities, media, and other external factors, which all begin to shape their evaluations and self-expression.

Practicing self-as-process can be highly effective in therapy. Guiding a client to notice their external or internal experiences in the present moment—step-by-step, as the content changes—helps interrupt habitual patterns of self-awareness and self-presentation.

2.1.2 Working with What Is Really There

Clients often enter therapy with a well-worn self-concept, behaving in ways that align with it. For many, practicing self-as-process initially feels unnatural. Exercises such as "What are you noticing now… and now… and what is coming up now…" are not how they typically engage with the world. However, becoming present almost always leads clients to notice something new. Oftentimes, the "persona" they present is designed to hide certain feelings or experiences. It's remarkable how a therapy session can unfold differently when self-as-process exercises are applied.

I recall one client who appeared disengaged and somewhat detached. When I asked her what she was experiencing in that moment, she immediately replied, "I would like to go." She then added, "I wasn't aware of that—this isn't how I usually feel when meeting with you." I acknowledged her courage and openness, and then gently asked her what she was experiencing now. She admitted to feeling insufficient, tied to a long-standing conflict with her mother, who had never acknowledged her efforts as good enough.

From that starting point, we worked with what was genuinely present. Together, we uncovered why she had wanted to leave—that topic was deeply uncomfortable for her, but ultimately worthwhile.

2.1.3 Distancing from Rigid Content

Developmentally, self-as-process begins without perspective-taking, as a young child lacks awareness of a continuous self. The child experiences sensations and emotions, but at first does not relate them to a past or future self, or to others—nor does the child evaluate these sensations and emotions. The ability of perspective-taking is acquired gradually over time. In therapy, when we practice self-as-process, we are typically working with adolescents or adults who have already developed the capacity of perspective-taking, which therefore naturally comes into play as well.

Awareness of self-as-process is essential for identifying specific thoughts or feelings, and recognizing that alternative thoughts, feelings, or perspectives are available. It provides a way to gain distance from rigid self-content, offering greater flexibility.

It's important to note that every experience, as part of self-as-process, is valid in reflecting the client's aliveness and perception. However, an experience does not always reflect the truth. For example, feeling scared doesn't necessarily mean there is actual danger. The experience might involve a racing heart, sweaty hands, or shaky knees—sensations we often label as "fear," depending on the context. The belief that one "is in a dangerous situation" is a conclusion drawn from that experience. Understanding and recognizing this distinction can be invaluable for clients, as it creates opportunities for them to respond to their feelings in new, more flexible ways.

Consider a person preparing for a presentation. They might notice, "My heart is pounding, my hands are sweaty, my knees are shaking." One interpretation could be: "I feel incredibly anxious about speaking in front of this group. That means it's too dangerous, so I won't do it." While the physical sensations are real, another person might interpret them as "big excitement" and think, "I'm thrilled and ready to speak to this group!"

Although both individuals experience similar bodily sensations, their interpretations and responses differ based on contextual factors such as their learning histories. The first person may have learned from an anxious caregiver to avoid public situations, while the second may have grown up with a parent who embraced performing on stage. Developing flexibility in interpretation can empower clients to explore new perspectives and try out alternative responses.

2.1.4 Taking Responsibility

Practicing self-awareness enables individuals to better understand their own preferences, needs, desires, and boundaries—which is essential for taking responsibility for their own well-being and living a fulfilled life. Oftentimes, we attribute our private experiences to the actions of others: "You lied to me, and that's why I feel bad." While lying is generally unacceptable and it's natural to feel hurt by it, there are various, more constructive ways to respond. For example:

- "I won't tolerate that. It's painful for me. What were you thinking?"
- "Can I count on you being honest in the future?"
- "I will distance myself from you, as this has happened repeatedly."

Sometimes, moving past disappointment takes time. However, remaining stuck in suffering—sometimes for years—is a personal response that reflects an important part of one's internal experience. Through self-as-process, you can guide your clients to become curious: "What's happening inside? What part of my response is preventing me from acting powerfully? Why do I feel so hurt that my ability to respond in a way that supports my own well-being seems unavailable? What external factors are contributing to me staying in this situation?"

2.1.5 Relevance for Therapy

Practicing self-as-process with your clients is an effective starting point when you notice a lack of flexibility, such as strong fusion with thoughts or avoidance of certain emotions.

This practice involves taking an experience as it is—a strong tension, sweaty palms, trembling knees—without immediately interpreting it or reacting to it.

To facilitate self-as-process, you might:

- Slow down the pace and guide the client to notice and name their present-moment perceptions. It is important to do this calmly yet fluidly, without getting stuck on any particular experience, while helping the client maintain awareness of their "I" in the here and now.
- Help the client recognize how they automatically label their experiences (e.g., as fear or excitement) and the conclusions they draw about their actions (e.g., avoiding a situation versus acknowledging it).

You can choose to focus on either of these two practices, combine them, or proceed to other processes, which often happens naturally. You can introduce perspective-taking to help the client create distance from their ongoing perceptions. When the client feels difficult emotions, you can practice acceptance. When they notice unhelpful actions, you can look at their values with them. This broader perspective empowers clients to make more intentional choices about how they genuinely want to act. Enhancing behavioral flexibility is central to this work.

Self-as-process work in therapy helps clients cultivate awareness of the intricate connections between bodily sensations, emotions, thoughts, and actions—which are unique to each individual. People often experience a sense of relief upon identifying their patterns and gaining a deeper understanding of themselves—and how they can motivate, free, or empower themselves to act in more satisfying and fulfilling ways.

2.2 Self-as-Content

As defined by researchers (McHugh et al., 2019, p. 106), self-as-content refers to "the conceptualized self, or self as the content of verbal relations. The conceptualized self is a well-elaborated relational network, one that includes every verbally known aspect of life and integrates one's knowledge of one's current and historical feelings, sensations, preferences, abilities, thoughts, interactions, and learning." More simply, self-as-content is the story we tell about ourselves—the concept of who we believe we are. This story is shaped by our experiences and our reactions to them, including actions, emotions, evaluations, and thoughts.

2.2.1 Distinguishing Self-as-Content and Self-Content

In clinical practice, the term self-as-content is often used to describe the rigid network of narratives or beliefs clients hold about themselves, which can keep them stuck in unhelpful patterns of behavior. These stories may hinder their long-term well-being across personal and professional contexts (e.g., "I am depressed," "I am an addict," "I am an anxious person," "I am aggressive").

Self-content, on the other hand, refers to the labels, roles, and characteristics we may adopt in different contexts. These can be helpful or unhelpful, valuable or not, temporary or long term. Think of them as "snippets" of self-as-content. However, they remain part of the conceptualized self, which encompasses all our experiences. For clarity, the term "rigid self-content" can be used synonymously with "self-as-content."

Self-content emerges through language, beginning when children start naming their experiences and identifying with those labels. This is when thoughts like "I am… [e.g., slow, popular, athletic, different]" first arise.

2.2.2 The Unavoidable Nature of Self-as-Content

As human beings, we cannot escape having self-content. Our personalities, experiences, dreams, and even our relationships with our bodies are shaped by language from the moment we begin to learn it. We are labeled and come to identify as little sister or big brother, sweet or nasty, girl, boy, not sure, something else, smart, stupid, tall, short, anxious, bold, too much of this, not enough of that, Swedish, Nepalese, our skin color, and so on.

Throughout development, we (hopefully) internalize useful rules from caregivers, such as "Respect your elders," "Stay warm," and "Don't cheat." These lessons may become part of our personality or, at the very least, our behavioral repertoire. At the same time, children can also absorb ideals from media, including journals, books, movies, and social media platforms, forming beliefs like "This is smart" or "This is how a popular person should behave."

All these bits and pieces form the vast network of self-as-content. Since the mind craves simplicity and coherence, this network organizes itself as coherently as possible—even if the resulting narrative isn't entirely accurate or helpful. In reality, most of us are far more complex: we can be both smart and foolish, embody both masculine and feminine traits, or feel outgoing in some situations and reserved in others, depending on the context. We naturally behave differently with close friends than with professional authorities, and even among different groups of friends or family members, we might express varying aspects of ourselves. Recognizing this complexity requires reflection and awareness, as it challenges the mind's preference for a simplified, consistent narrative.

However, certain incidents can solidify into rigid, limiting self-as-content due to some downsides of the language process.

2.2.3 An Example

Imagine a child innocently raising her hand in first grade to ask her teacher a question. The teacher responds dismissively, "That's a stupid question," and the classmates laugh. The child is unlikely to remember this event as "I asked one question in first grade, and the teacher thought it was stupid." Instead, she may internalize it as "I am stupid" or "I shouldn't have asked that question." This memory can become associated with unpleasant emotions like shame, sadness, or anger. At that age, the child likely lacks the capacity to reflect and ask, "How do I want to deal with this painful experience of being publicly shamed?" Instead, she will instinctively cope with the pain in whatever way feels manageable in the moment. Children have limited options, and even many adults remain unaware that they can choose how to respond to their mental or emotional challenges.

For example, a child who experiences public shaming might start thinking, "I will never ask a question publicly again," which could later evolve into, "I should hide how stupid I am." This is what we call a "rule"—in short, an instruction that "prescribes behavior" (Törneke, 2010, p. 113).

The ability to derive such rules is a remarkable capacity of the mind, allowing us to avoid repeating mistakes and even learn from others' experiences (e.g., don't place your hand on a hot stove). However, as the child's example shows, such rules can also limit the range of possible actions. Most rules operate implicitly, meaning we are often unaware of their influence. This makes it harder for individuals to evaluate whether their rules genuinely help them live the life they want for themselves. For instance, later in life, the person who was shamed as a child might notice that she feels cautious and anxious in groups, even though she genuinely wishes to trust others and speak up. Her behavioral repertoire has become restricted, obstructing her ability to pursue a fulfilling life.

Experiences tend to accumulate and reinforce themselves, narrowing a person's perceptions and interpretations. The person might reliably notice experiences that confirm her self-concept of being "stupid" while overlooking moments of competence or intelligence. The more she avoids situations that provoke fear, the stronger her perceptions of threat and shame might become. After sidestepping a challenging situation, she might think, "I'm glad I didn't speak up—it would have been a disaster." This avoidance prevents her from challenging the underlying rule and creating alternative, more empowering experiences. Over time, this pattern can leave her feeling stuck and silenced, thinking, "This is how I am."

Self-as-content can feel like being trapped in a spiderweb of language. Each new experience strengthens the web, making it harder to see beyond the story and limiting opportunities for growth and change.

2.2.4 Relevance for Therapy

The clinical relevance of self-as-content is immediately apparent, as it is mostly constraining narratives that bring clients to therapy. In fact, self-as-content is likely the first aspect of the self that stands out when meeting a new client ("I feel misunderstood by people around me," "I am burned out," "I am an autist," "When I present in my professional context, I get mute and forget what to say.").

Clients often seek help to change their self-content, believing that replacing negative narratives with positive ones—such as "I am valuable" instead of "I am worthless"—will resolve their struggles. However, changing content is not our primary therapeutic approach, as additional content would not necessarily result in more flexible, adaptive action. Instead, we have more effective tools, such as becoming aware of rigid self-content, gaining some distance from it, and considering new actions.

The main clinical point is that self-as-content fosters rigid behaviors by narrowing perception and creating unhelpful cycles of internal experiences and actions. This is where our clinical work begins—not with trying to change self-content itself, but by addressing the processes that sustain it. When therapy is effective, new self-content naturally evolves as clients expand their behavioral options and develop a sense of self-efficacy.

As a therapist, you can support your clients by:

- Helping them identify limiting self-content that they apply indiscriminately, across all contexts, even when it may not be appropriate.
- Using perspective-taking to help them develop a broader perspective on difficult self-content, connect it to a meaningful life direction, or cultivate self-compassion.

- Guiding them to identify and accept the obstructive thoughts and emotions that arise with new steps, so they are not held back by such thoughts and emotions.
- Encouraging them to push their boundaries in small, manageable steps in contexts where doing so feels beneficial to them.

This process is not easy. Confronting painful experiences and stepping into the unknown can be one of life's most daunting challenges. Yet, it is also essential for achieving greater freedom. It's like maintaining a home: dust will accumulate on its own, but the house won't clean itself. Taking deliberate action is necessary.

Practicing self-as-process can help interrupt a person's entanglement with self-as-content. By focusing on the present moment—what is happening here and now—clients develop a greater awareness of the actual context. Other therapeutic processes, such as acceptance and connecting with values, are equally important. Challenging and disrupting the conceptualized self can evoke pain and anxiety, making these supportive processes critical.

For example, consider the person who developed the belief that asking questions in a group is dangerous and decided to hide her perceived "stupidity." As an adult, this belief might influence her perceptions in a professional training group, causing her to view others as critical rather than kind and welcoming. Her internal focus may remain on their anxiety or on thoughts like "I should already know this; this will be another stupid question."

In contrast, a broader goal or value—such as "I want to trust this group because we share the same aim of gaining professional knowledge"—might not even come to mind.

If this person is open to having a new experience, she could now practice self-as-process and perspective-taking. For instance, she might carefully observe the group members to determine whether they appear genuinely hostile or rather open. She could recall whether others had asked questions and how those questions were received. Additionally, she could ground herself with mindful breathing and by allowing her feelings to be present. She might assess the risk of being shamed and weigh it against the potential insights to be gained from asking her question. She might even realize that the courage to ask the question and challenge old restrictions could, in itself, make trying something new worthwhile.

She could then ask herself, "What is most important to me in this situation?" and make a conscious choice. The choice might be: "I am not willing to risk being shamed again, so I won't ask this question now." Or: "I want to speak up in the group and dare to be visible with what I don't know, because gaining better professional skills is important to me." The latter choice might require her to face and work through feelings of shame, fear, or other emotions that may arise in the moment. By repeatedly acting in this way, she may gradually overcome the painful memory from her school years and reclaim a sense of freedom.

When someone wants to break free from automatic behaviors but hesitates to do so, we can describe this as "being stuck." In these moments, adopting a broader perspective will often help. A good first step is to notice and allow being stuck—bringing awareness to it and practicing willingness to experience it. While this may feel uncomfortable, it opens the door to accessing a larger perspective: the observer self. Paradoxically, the grounded acknowledgment of "This is where I am, and I allow myself to be here" often creates space to be more creative and identify small, actionable steps forward.

2.3 Self-as-Context

According to McHugh et al. (2019, p. 106), self-as-context is "the observing self, or self as the context of verbal relations." They also describe it as "a verbal category that applies to everything a person has ever done," and that "incorporates both the nonverbal self (the behavioral stream resulting from direct psychological processes) and the verbal self (as both object and process of knowledge gained through relational framing). Thus, self-as-context has been described as providing the experiential link between nonverbal and verbal self-knowledge." (2019, p. 115)

In other literature, self-as-context is referred to as "self-as-perspective" (Törneke, 2010), "perspective-taking self" (Hayes et al., 2020), "observer perspective," "self-view" (Ciarocchi, 2022), or "theory of mind" (Hayes & Hofmann, 2023).

This perspective "does not change once it emerges" (Hayes, 1995, p. 96). It is the vantage point that remains constant across time, place, and content—the transcendent perspective of I-here-now. We cannot observe this permanent perspective directly, we can only become aware that we are observing from it. It is "the behavior of seeing that you see from a particular locus or perspective" (Hayes, 1984, p. 102).

Unlike self-as-content (what we think we are) or self-as-process (what we feel or do in the moment), self-as-context refers to the perspective from which all of these are observed.

Simply put, self-as-context represents "the experience of human consciousness" (Hayes, 2024). We might also describe self-as-context as becoming aware of the context of all our experiences ("who is noticing that") (Rainer Sonntag, 2024, personal conversation).

2.3.1 Key Aspects of Self-as-Context

1. PERSPECTIVE-TAKING: A STABLE PLACE FROM WHICH ONE EXPERIENCES

Perspective-taking serves as the foundational ability upon which this third aspect of the self is built. It refers to "the ability to attribute mental states to oneself and to understand that others have beliefs, desires, intentions, and perspectives that differ from one's own" (Hayes et al., 2020, p. 31).

It involves recognizing:

- That all experiences are encountered from a personal point of view—"I-here-now"
- While also understanding that others simultaneously experience the world from their own "I-here-now"

Taking a perspective on oneself and others is—besides self-as-process—a foundational requirement for developing a sense of self. In this way, perspective-taking is regarded as a uniquely human capacity—one that "confers a flexibility that is particularly important for psychological health" (McHugh et al., 2019, p. 116).

Perspective-taking allows us to turn toward our thoughts, feelings, or bodily experiences with openness and distance, rather than being carried away by them ("I am looking at this thought or feeling, and I decide what to do next."). We establish a space of awareness that allows us to consciously choose our next actions, rather than reacting automatically to our experiences.

2. HIERARCHICAL PERSPECTIVE: INTEGRATING EXPERIENCES

The hierarchical perspective emphasizes the context in which all our experiences occur, the constant point of awareness. It allows not only distance, but also the integration of everything we think, feel, experience, and do. All of this belongs to us—and yet, we are more than the sum of these parts. Since all experiences can be observed, there must be something—our consciousness—that holds it all.

The hierarchical perspective highlights a broader, overarching awareness—integrating elements such as values, purpose, kindness, and compassion.

We can see the hierarchical perspective as emerging through practicing perspective-taking, looking from I-here-now at multiple objects, thoughts, feelings, bodily experiences, or roles, experiencing that the point of awareness, "I" is always the same (email discussion, Peer Reviewed Trainers Listserve, 2024).

Evidence suggests that incorporating the hierarchical perspective provides significant advantages in clinical work, compared to focusing solely on the perspective of distinction (Hayes et al., 2020; Styles & Atkins, 2018; Yu, McCracken, & Norton, 2016; Zettle et al., 2018), which aligns with clinical experience.

In clinical work, the focus is on facilitating the lived experience of this stable perspective, rather than merely acquiring conceptual knowledge or belief.

2.3.2 The Nature of Self-as-Context

Self-as-context does not evaluate experiences but provides the space to encompass all experiences and evaluations that arise. For instance, self-as-context (if it could talk) wouldn't say, "I am furious, and this is bad." Instead, it might say, "I notice that I am furious, and I notice that I evaluate this as bad. And all of that is part of myself, one possible action among many others." The perspective of I-here-now allows us to observe our own experiences (I-there-now or I-there-then) without becoming entangled in them.

In essence, self-as-context is simple: you can feel your body right now, sitting in a chair and reading this text. At the same time, you can also notice yourself feeling your body, sitting the chair, and reading. However, grasping this abstract perspective can be challenging. To make it more accessible, we often use experiential metaphors. Some classical ones are:

- An observer looking at oneself.
- A chessboard providing space for the game.
- The sky, always present, whether it's cloudy or clear.

Self-as-context is a conscious action, always practiced from the perspective of I-here-now. While we can imagine other people's perspectives or moments in time (e.g., "I think my friend feels upset," or "I remember attending that concert last year"), this imagination still arises from I-here-now. Every human being embodies a unique perspective shaped by their bodily sensations, learning history, culture, genetics, environment, and numerous other contextual factors.

The observer perspective as a conscious practice must be distinguished from a more automatic critical self-perspective—for example, when clients recall past situations, see themselves in their mind's eye, and ruminate about not having behaved well. This kind of perspective, often dominant in people with mental difficulties, has also been referred to as an "observer perspective" in scientific literature (Kuyken & Moulds, 2009).

It is important to differentiate between these two modes, because the critical self-perspective often reinforces entanglement with negative self-evaluations, while the conscious observer perspective fosters greater freedom and flexibility.

We can practice observing our experiences from the perspective of I-here-now, either by witnessing the experiences directly—like a person behind a camera, observing what unfolds—or by noticing ourselves as the one having the experience—like seeing ourselves in front of the camera, as part of the scene.

We can also recall memories and form evaluations from either viewpoint.

However, memories rooted in a critical self-perspective—as opposed to memories of direct observation—have been associated with "greater negative self-evaluation, lower dispositional mindfulness, and greater use of avoidance," (Kuyken & Moulds, 2009, p. 624).

In the context of this book, such automatic, self-critical memories are not considered part of the observer perspective as we define it. Instead, they are understood as elements of self-as-content.

Practicing self-as-context in relation to such critical self-memories involves shifting the perspective by asking, "Who is noticing these evaluations and memories?" In doing so, we create space to observe them as experiences, while recognizing that we are more than these thoughts or memories.

2.3.3 Learning Perspective-Taking

As children gradually develop perspective-taking, they begin to understand that they are not the center of the world and that others have their own points of view. Alongside the growing awareness of "I" or "me" comes the awareness of "you," as the two are intrinsically connected (McHugh et al., 2019)—like the front and back of a hand.

Learning perspective-taking enables children to move beyond immediate impulses like "I want these sweets now!" and the subsequent tantrums when their desires aren't met. Over time, they might realize that "I" not screaming in the supermarket now could result in mom being more generous later (then), leading to even more sweets. They may also begin to take their mother's perspective (I-here-now looking at her-there-then), understanding that a public outburst might embarrass her and that they don't want to get her in trouble.

However, just because children develop the ability to take perspectives doesn't mean they always apply it—and this is true for adults as well.

Perspective-taking allows children to learn how they appear in a social context ("That kid laughed at me, so I must be funny") and to recognize what behaviors are effective or ineffective ("If I let my friend copy my homework, she likes me more—but the teacher scolds me"). It also helps them understand themselves in relation to others ("Dad is upset because I played 'snow' with flour in the kitchen," or "I feel happy when Mom hugs me, but I feel lonely when she leaves for a business trip"). Through perspective-taking, children can imagine scenarios that haven't occurred yet ("I wish my mom would come back") and empathize with others by imagining their feelings ("It must feel bad for this boy to be scolded").

With perspective-taking, children begin to evaluate and reflect on their own experiences, compare themselves to others, and recognize others' reactions. For example:

- "My friend said he doesn't like me anymore, and that makes me sad."
- "I love eating ice cream, but it's not good because it has a lot of sugar."
- "I'm good at playing football and can run faster than anyone else on the team."
- "I get angry when my sister takes my toys, but Dad says I shouldn't be angry."

This ability also helps children better predict how others will react and adjust their behavior accordingly (e.g., "My teacher always gets angry when someone talks in class, so maybe I better stay quiet now"). Children begin to create self-instructions and rules (e.g., "That person cheated me—I'll never trust them again!"), which has a downside, as these rules can become unhelpful and overly restrictive in the long term.

On the other hand, applying perspective-taking can help individuals gain flexibility with their self-knowledge. For instance, a child might think, "I believe I'm stupid, but my teacher says my answers are correct. Maybe I'm not entirely stupid, and I can learn more." This capacity to step back and see oneself from a broader perspective is one of the main advantages of self-as-context (McHugh et al., 2019).

2.3.4 Adopting the Hierarchical Perspective

When development progresses well and individuals have plenty of learning opportunities, the hierarchical perspective on the self can emerge—an awareness that one is more than their self-content. This perspective allows individuals not only to distance themselves from self-content, but also to view themselves from a broader point of view. For example, it can enable them to see their values as overarching, comprehensive guides for their lives, and encourage actions aligned with these values.

The broader perspective also fosters self-compassion, helping individuals reframe challenging current events or childhood experiences with kindness. These experiences can simultaneously be seen as both connected to and separate from the self, which aids in their acceptance and integration (e.g., "I can look at this challenging experience now, it happened in my past and it is over—it's a part of me, but I am more than that. I can handle it.").

Furthermore, self-as-context nurtures deeper compassion for others, facilitating the ability to adopt another's perspective and connect with them more fully—whether by sharing moments of great joy or profound loss.

2.3.5 A Discrete Event for Humanity

Hayes and Hofmann (2023) describe the evolutionary emergence of higher levels of human consciousness, grounded in language abilities, as a "discrete event" for humanity, granting our species significant advantages such as cooperation and the creation of culture. They identify several "key features" evolving from human consciousness, including "meta-cognitive awareness; awareness of awareness; self-monitoring; meta-representation; global availability; construction of a sense of self, both a core self and social self; and the experiential aspects of consciousness" (Hayes & Hofmann, 2023, p. 6).

For contemporary challenges, Hayes and Hoffman see great potential for advancing therapy by leveraging these features. They suggest that these abilities stem from the continuous practice of processes we have previously discussed, such as naming objects, labeling private experiences, talking about oneself, drawing conclusions from past events, or simultaneously taking the perspectives of "me" and "you." Therefore, therapy becomes most effective when it is grounded in these fundamental processes.

By cultivating distance from and awareness of self-content, clients can achieve a clearer and more transparent understanding of themselves. Sometimes, this hierarchical perspective manifests as sudden insights, such as, "Wow, this isn't really the truth about me!" or "Oh, this is who I'm meant to be." It may also emerge as a profound sense of connectedness or oneness—what some might describe as a spiritual experience or something beyond words.

Meditation practices often nurture and strengthen self-as-context skills, and I encourage clients who have access to spiritual practices to explore them. Likewise, psychedelic-assisted therapy—when conducted by experienced clinicians in a safe, controlled environment—can facilitate self-as-context experiences, especially for individuals facing exceptionally difficult circumstances (Hayes et al., 2020; Luoma, Sabucedo, Eriksson, Gates, & Pilecki, 2019).

Applying perspective-taking exercises can help foster the transcendent aspects of self-as-context when appropriate for the client. However, in my view, experiencing these moments is more of a gift than a goal. They are neither mandatory for effective clinical work nor the primary focus of this practical book. And yet, they may unfold or become meaningful for some clients (or for us as clinicians).

2.3.6 Relevance for Therapy

In therapy, self-as-context relies on two key abilities:

- Perspective-taking by practicing I-you, here-there, and now-then relations with all kinds of objects, persons, or internal or external experiences.
- Fostering a hierarchical perspective by asking questions like "Who is noticing all of that?" and using other targeted interventions.

This training is intended to introduce some helpful disruption or foster flexibility in a client's self-concept. It's easy to make self-as-context experiential for clients. You might ask something like:

- "Can you feel your body, how it is sitting in the chair, listening to me?" (self-as-process)
- "And can you also become aware that you feel your body, sitting in the chair, listening to me?" and "Who is noticing that?" (self-as-context)

These questions help clients connect with their observer perspective.

PRACTICING THE PERSPECTIVE OF I-YOU

You might also ask, "You see me, sitting there in front of you, listening to you. How is it to become aware of that? How does it feel?" Perhaps the client feels relaxed or tense, safe or something else. The focus is not so much on the specific content of their experience as on getting them to practice noticing and sharing the own perspective—in this case connecting with "I" and "you."

Clients will hopefully experience a nonjudgmental space where everything can be expressed—including, for instance, "I notice that I don't feel safe." Practicing perspective-taking will help you, as the therapist, not take such disclosures personally. Instead, you can approach them with curiosity and reinforce openness by saying something like: "Thank you for sharing that and being open with me. What do you notice now, as you shared it and I responded?" In this way, perspective-taking can be a powerful tool for nurturing the therapeutic relationship.

PRACTICING THE PERSPECTIVE OF NOW-THEN

All experiences occur in the present moment—there is no moment other than the one unfolding right now. You might try it yourself: Please pause for a breath or two and notice that you are reading this now. You can't read five minutes ago; you can only recall that you read something five minutes ago. And when you read something an hour from now, it will still be the "now" of that moment. So, there is only this moment, and everything else is either a memory or a projection into the future. Is there anything else you notice when you do this little exercise?

You can invent similar exercises with your clients. The moment you and your client share together is the only real moment in both of your lives. Helping clients become aware of this fact can profoundly impact the therapeutic process.

There are many additional ways to explore how perspective on time can be utilized in therapy. When a difficult feeling arises, you can work with the client to examine how it feels in the present moment ("now") and whether they have experienced it at another time ("then"). Together, you can explore the current context and compare it to the context of the past. You can also ask how this difficult feeling would show up, if you were thinking back on it in ten years from now. Any guided exploration like this can help foster greater integration of the painful feeling.

PRACTICING THE PERSPECTIVE OF HERE-THERE

We and our bodies are always here and now. This is why bringing awareness to the body immediately anchors us in the present moment. While the mind can wander anywhere at any time, the body cannot. We rarely stop to consider it, but our sense of "I" is deeply connected to our body. I often guide my clients to become aware of their bodies, helping them realize that they live within their bodies, that their bodies are uniquely theirs, and that they cannot be separate from their body. They come to see that they wouldn't be "here" without their body and that no other body is available to them. The body is always "here."

No matter where they are, when clients point to themselves, they find themselves "here." Once they recognize "here," they also observe that most other things—including their therapist—are "there." When asked about thoughts and emotions, "Do you experience this thought/feeling here or there?" they typically perceive these experiences as "here," which can make them more challenging to handle. Thoughts and emotions often feel like an unchangeable part of the self, similar to the body. Because they are so close ("here"), they can become particularly bothersome.

Introducing a hierarchical perspective by asking, "Who is noticing this thought/feeling?" can create a sense of distance, allowing clients to shift from experiencing the body, thought, or emotion as "I-here-now" to observing it as "I-there-now." This shift provides space to consciously engage with and better manage these experiences.

You can foster this awareness through mindfulness exercises, highlighting aspects such as autonomy ("You are sitting here because you chose to sit here"), values ("What is so important to you that you are here?"), or other elements relevant to the client's context. The same insights and distinctions can be seamlessly woven into therapeutic conversations as well.

HIERARCHICAL PERSPECTIVE

"When we emphasize the client's direct experience of self-as-context, we build a stable and transcendent place from which it is possible to work and from which self as a process of knowing can honestly go on." (Hayes, 1995, p. 96)

The aforementioned exercises for perspective-taking can be steps to establish the hierarchical perspective. A useful exercise to foster the hierarchical perspective more directly is to ask clients to recall a situation from a few days ago, from their young adulthood, and from their childhood. In each instance, guide them to recognize that their observer perspective must have been present—otherwise, they would not be able to recall those moments.

You can similarly guide clients to reflect on the different roles they play in life and how those roles change over time, while their observer perspective remains constant. You can direct their attention to their body, thoughts, and feelings, and let them notice how these aspects change constantly. Then, ask if they can notice that the only consistent element across all these situations is the observer perspective. This exploration can be woven into the conversation or extended into a longer exercise (see the original exercise in Hayes, Strosahl, & Wilson, 2004). What's important is not simply conveying abstract knowledge, but rather giving clients a direct, experiential understanding of the observer perspective.

CLINICAL PROCESS OF USING SELF-ASPECTS

An example of the clinical process of working with self-aspects might unfold as follows:

Clients begin by perceiving and naming private experiences in the moment (self-as-process). This often leads to a heightened awareness of difficult content (self-as-content, perspective-taking). You can then guide them to accept these challenging experiences when appropriate and explore their context (acceptance, perspective-taking). Clients practice not only opening up to the content but also creating distance from it (further perspective-taking). A subsequent step might involve helping clients integrate this content as part of themselves—recognizing it as an important aspect that has shaped their self-image—while also realizing that they are much more than this content (self-as-context).

Of course, this process is not linear. Each part can be addressed individually and revisited as needed. It often involves cycles of progress and regression, with clients moving back and forth through these stages in dynamic loops.

2.4 Conclusion

The three self-aspects described in this chapter—self-as-process, self-as-content, and self-as-context—have proven to be invaluable in clinical practice and training. They are not meant to provide a comprehensive theoretical model of the self, nor do they fully align with precise scientific terminology. However, there is robust empirical support for their practical relevance (McHugh et al.,

2019), with further research continuing to expand our understanding of these subtle and complex processes.

Self-as-context is particularly powerful in teaching clients something that may initially seem paradoxical: how to create distance from their thoughts, feelings, and bodily sensations, so they are not consumed by them, while simultaneously embracing these experiences as valid and integral parts of themselves. For example, a client might realize, "Wow, I'm really furious right now," and instead of being overwhelmed by their anger, they can pause and ask, "What do I truly want to do next?"

Through self-as-context exercises, clients can learn to derive valuable insights from their painful experiences, gaining a deeper understanding of their vulnerabilities, limitations, and core aspirations. They no longer need to avoid or suppress certain emotions, but instead can allow those emotions, evaluate what is within their control, and choose to respond in ways that align with their values and promote their well-being. This approach fosters resilience, conserving energy previously spent on avoidance and rigid behavioral patterns, and helps clients reconnect with themselves to reclaim their sense of agency.

Self-as-context, or the ability to observe ourselves, is often described as "transcendent" because it is ever-present throughout our lives. Free from content, it represents a stable perspective and accompanies us through every age we've been, every role we've taken on, every emotion, sensation, goal, or dream. Without it, we wouldn't even be able to recall past experiences, as remembering requires the sense of having been present and aware. Sometimes, we may experience a moment of pure awareness of that space from which we observe everything unfolding in our lives.

It is essential, however, to understand that self-as-context is not static. While the term "observer" might evoke the image of something fixed—like a detached entity hovering above—it is a perspective and an active, ongoing process. Self-as-context is a skill that can be cultivated and trained, continually evolving throughout life. It is never a finished capacity.

You may now begin to see how the three aspects of self are interconnected in different ways. For instance, self-as-process inherently involves self-content, as every momentary experience—such as "I am upset"—is also content. Not all momentary content becomes a defining part of the self. Over time, the practice of perceiving and naming one's experiences in the moment naturally generates new, hopefully more helpful self-content. Self-as-process often leads to perspective-taking. It is through distinctions like "I" versus "other," "now" versus "another time," and "here" versus "somewhere else" that we make sense of our experiences. Furthermore, practicing self-as-context incorporates the capacity of self-as-process and invites reflection on self-as-content.

While these three aspects are closely related, each has a distinct focus, making them each uniquely valuable in clinical work. Practical applications of these aspects—such as assessing flexibility in each aspect and engaging in targeted exercises—will be explored in the chapters ahead.

Through these self-aspects, we experience the self as a continuous, ever-evolving stream of perceptions (e.g., "I am confused"), responses to those perceptions (e.g., "I am a professional; I shouldn't feel confused—I should know this"), and responses to those responses (e.g., "I am being too hard on myself").

If you wish, take the next thirty seconds to tune into your own stream of experiences and simply notice it as it unfolds...

2.5 Summary

In this chapter, we looked at three aspects of the self that provide a valuable framework for understanding the self, and have proven to be relevant in clinical practice and training:

1. Self-as-Process
   Self-as-process refers to the ability to recognize and label what one experiences as "I" or "me" in the present moment, as well as what is observed outside oneself (e.g., "I am hungry," "I'm happy," "I hear bells ringing," "I walk"). Self-as-process emphasizes perception.
2. Self-as-Content
   Self-as-content represents the narrative a person tells about themselves—the "truth" they believe about who they are (e.g., "I am a greedy person," "I am a problem solver," "I am sensitive"). These self-concepts often keep people stuck in unhelpful patterns of internal experiences and associated actions (e.g., "I think I'm an unlikable person, so I won't go to this party"—the person therefore won't create new experiences).
3. Self-as-Context
   Self-as-context reflects the capacity to observe oneself, to become aware of oneself, to notice from the position of "I-here-now" what one is experiencing (self-as-process) or the self-story one is telling (self-as-content).

Self-as-context includes:

- Perspective-taking: Distinguishing I vs. you, here vs. there, now vs. then
- Hierarchical perspectives: Taking an overarching view on oneself, or adding broader perspectives like values, self-compassion, and compassion

Perspective-taking allows a person to gain distance from their self-content. The hierarchical perspective enables not only distance from self-content but also its integration.

Self-as-context is inherently social—it develops within a social context and is, in essence, a social capacity. Strong self-as-context skills support conscious, long-term, and values-driven responses both in relationship with ourselves and in social situations.

All three aspects of the self are actions and lifelong practices, not fixed entities. While they are closely related, each has a distinct emphasis that is clinically significant.

Practicing new perspectives and related actions can help generate fresh, more supportive self-content, allowing individuals to break free from restrictive narratives.

> The observer perspective works by allowing me to view the negative aspects of the illness (shattered dreams, life with obstacles and pain, etc.) from a neutral, external standpoint and consider how I can still create a fulfilling life. Seeing things from the outside helps to reassess situations, redefine goals, and discover new dreams that are still possible despite the illness.
>
> —Anja, thirty years old, teacher in early retirement

CHAPTER 3

Self-as-Context and a Pivot

In the ACT model, there are more processes besides self-as-context that are essential for a healthy lifestyle, and we cannot fully comprehend self-as-context without considering them.

The six so-called core processes are defined as follows:

- Self-as-context: Awareness of our own noticing and of the vantage point from which we are noticing
- Defusion: Choosing which thoughts to give importance to and which ones to not
- Acceptance: Acknowledging and allowing experiences to be as they are in a certain moment, especially our emotions
- Presence: Perceiving what is happening around us or within us
- Values: Identifying what truly matters to us
- Committed action: Engaging in alignment with our values

Mastering these processes is seen as the heart of mental and behavioral health for human beings.

These processes are also strongly interconnected, and we can gradually consider which process might be most helpful for a specific client in a particular situation and moment.

A person's ability to flexibly and appropriately apply these six processes, rather than rigidly repeating the same often-unfavorable behaviors, determines the extent to which they experience a sense of choice and self-efficacy in life. We would say that practicing these six processes leads to greater psychological and behavioral flexibility.

Steven C. Hayes, the originator of ACT, identifies deep-seated yearnings or intrinsic motivations as underlying each of the six core processes (Hayes, 2019).

Following your yearnings means, in short, moving toward:

- Self-as-context: Being seen and cared for, and finding a sense of belonging with yourself and others
- Defusion: Creating a coherent understanding of yourself and your life
- Acceptance: Feeling and experiencing your own vitality
- Presence: Orienting yourself to where you are
- Values: Determining valuable life directions
- Committed action: Developing competence to follow these life directions

Instead of classifying specific symptoms as pathological and abnormal, this model sees harmful behavior as a failure to follow the yearnings in a context-sensitive way and to experience the desired sense of fulfillment.

Yearnings can serve as healthy guides, but they may also lead to rigid attachments and inflexible behavior, leaving a person feeling stuck. For example, a person might develop perfectionism, striving to avoid failure to maintain an image of competence. They might ignore important divergent perspectives to keep up a coherent picture of themself or their life. Or they might distort themself in an effort to feel seen or feel a sense of belonging within a group.

When working with clients caught in such patterns, exploring their learning history and current context can reveal the underlying functions of these behaviors. Often, these patterns are repeated without ever satisfying the core yearnings—and, in many cases, they even hinder the achievement of the desired outcomes. But crucially, they still serve an important and desirable purpose.

Hayes's perspective flips our understanding of mental illness and provides therapists with new interventions that are less stigmatizing for people seeking support. Mostly, this means helping your clients to open up to their pain, so they can redirect their original motivation toward what matters to them. Hayes refers to this step as a "pivot," a turning point that helps individuals move in a new direction, toward what they genuinely desire.

In this chapter, you will learn about self-as-context in relation to each of the six flexibility processes and what it looks like to get stuck in a dead end. You will also see ways to bring about the pivot, to move toward the yearning once again.

3.1 Exploring the Pivots with a Client Case

A client named Fanny came to me after a deeply painful experience where she fell in love "for the first time in her life." Her previous relationships had been enjoyable flings, but now, in her late thirties, she had discovered a passion she had never felt before. Sadly, it turned into a disaster, leaving her with significant financial losses and, even more devastating, a profound loss of self-esteem.

Fanny was a successful lawyer and had always seen herself as an independent and cheerful woman. Now, she found herself deceived—financially and romantically, as the man had been involved with other women. She could barely believe it. Although she had ended the relationship, she was consumed by shame and disappointment in herself for letting it happen. Determined to avoid ever experiencing such pain again, she resolved never to fall in love again.

She longed to reclaim her old, confident, and independent self, desperately fighting to rid herself of the pain. She denied how deeply she was hurting, threw herself into work to avoid feeling it, and began drinking too much wine alone in her apartment after work. She refused to admit that she still missed the man.

She wasn't able to orient herself in the new situation of betrayal and devaluation. She had no sense of being cared for, nor of belonging, as she was hiding her situation even from her close friends. Fanny denied the depth of her pain and clung to her coherent image of herself (successful and independent) and of men (to be kept at a distance, otherwise they would hurt her).

Disconnected from what truly mattered to her, her energy was consumed by avoidance strategies (overworking and drinking). Yet, despite all this, she felt stuck—desperately searching for a way to break free from her turmoil.

This brought Fanny into therapy. We started to work on giving more space to the hurt and considering what could make her pain—which she described as "unbearable"—feel worth enduring. For her, it was the possibility of inner peace and freedom—something she realized she had never truly experienced. She recognized that she had always felt dependent on working hard, being successful, and proving her worth.

Her health deteriorated. For weeks, she struggled to get out of bed in the morning, neglected her appearance, ate very little, and experienced suicidal thoughts.

At one point, Fanny revealed that as a child, she had witnessed her violent father nearly kill her mother. Despite the abuse, her mother stayed in the relationship, feeling powerless against her husband's attacks. While her father was not physically violent toward Fanny, he would shout at her daily, calling her "bad and useless" and criticizing her every move. Minutes later, he would tell her how much he loved her and how important she was to him. Fanny confessed, "I thought it was normal to be treated like that."

She had carried deep shame over enduring this treatment for decades, as her father's behavior continued into her adult life. He was her only family member left, as her mother had passed away early. For Fanny, love and abuse had become inseparably linked. My hypothesis was that she had tried to escape this painful dynamic in her relationships by staying guarded with men and keeping them at a distance. Yet, when she finally opened her heart, she found herself drawn to a man who fit the same destructive pattern.

However, examining this harmful relationship openly with the guidance of a therapist became her path to healing. Step by step, after painful weeks, she was able to let go of her self-image of being successful but unapproachable. She allowed her vulnerability and the full extent of her pain to emerge in our therapy sessions. As one outcome, she stayed in contact with her father without resentment. But when he started yelling at her, she ended the conversation.

Confronting her own helplessness as a child was the most challenging part of her journey. In our sessions, she dared to feel those emotions. She learned not to be swept away by the pain, but rather to care for it, just like a mother would care for her child. Through hard work, she began practicing self-as-context. And for the first time in her life, she felt free. She said she no longer feared falling into the same trap again with a new partner. She knew that she would have painful experiences, but she had learned to trust her ability to deal with them.

3.2 Self-as-Context: Yearning for Belonging and Connection

Within the domain of the self, our deepest yearning is to connect, belong, and be seen for our uniqueness (Hayes, 2019). Babies develop their sense of self in tandem with their caregivers, receiving supportive feedback for their natural self-expression (Beebe et al., 2019).

In Fanny's case, her trust in others was limited. She avoided belonging and resisted being seen in her vulnerability. Growing up with an abusive father and a mother trapped in a violent relationship, she likely had few opportunities to learn what a safe, secure relationship looks like. She discovered early on that achieving good grades was the only way to gain her father's attention, leading her to adopt a pattern of overworking at a young age.

Fanny became disconnected from her inner experiences, as no one showed interest in them. She became trapped in a rigid self-concept ("Something must be wrong with me if I'm treated like this"), unspoken rules ("I must avoid closeness with men to avoid being hurt"), comparisons to others ("Everyone else has a family; I'm a failure"), and idealized standards ("I have to be the best to earn attention"). Ultimately, these patterns left her feeling lonely and isolated.

3.2.1 The Pivot of Self-as-Context

The pivotal step toward a more flexible and fulfilling life in the realm of self involves helping clients view themselves as whole, multifaceted individuals—with all their aspects, including flaws, strengths, and vulnerabilities. This process requires courage and practice because it involves confronting the pain they had previously avoided: the pain of not receiving the love, acceptance, and safe space they needed for the confident unfolding of their selves; the pain of feeling rejected, flawed, or wronged. It can be deeply challenging and even threatening when one's self-image begins to crumble, which is why it's essential to let clients control the pace of this work.

The pivot of self-as-context encourages clients to continually become present with themselves: "This is me, just as I am in this moment. I may not like it, but I consciously acknowledge it and give it space." In doing so, they begin to reconnect with themselves and better understand both their challenges and their true needs.

For Fanny, this meant expanding her self-image by embracing her vulnerability—something she had long despised. Allowing herself to feel that pain revealed the urgency of setting boundaries against her father's verbal abuse, and it gave her the strength to act.

Your presence as a therapist can create a safe space for clients to take these transformative steps. By helping them perceive that you are attentively present—by asking questions like, "Are you aware that I am here with you? That I am interested in you? Do you feel safe with me to explore this?"—you can help clients find relief in a genuine, compassionate connection.

This experience of authentic contact not only supports clients in becoming more mindfully connected with themselves, but also provides a model for engaging with others. As they practice this mindful presence in their everyday lives, they may begin to experience healthier, more fulfilling relationships.

3.3 Defusion: Yearning for Coherence

The process of defusion involves creating distance between oneself and one's thoughts. This concept is so central to ACT that acceptance and commitment therapy was initially called "cognitive distancing."

When faced with problems, we often become entangled in our thoughts, cycling through endless loops of hypothetical solutions. Most of us are trained to solve problems by thinking, and as a result, the mind often takes on the role of a self-proclaimed boss, declaring: "I am the pinnacle of creation; I can predict and solve all your problems; I have answers to all your questions." Unfortunately, this is far from the truth. Our mind frequently predicts problems that never occur, and it is not particularly skilled at solving emotional issues. Instead, the mind offers "good" advice—such as in Fanny's case: "Think more about what you did wrong to make your partner treat you so poorly; if you figure it out, you can prevent it from happening again."

Fanny assumed it was normal to be verbally abused by her father; she never questioned his behavior. In her harmful relationship, she recognized that her partner's actions were unacceptable, but the mistreatment was coherent with her prior experiences, making it feel validating on some level.

Additionally, Fanny ignored her emotional pain for a long time because she desperately wanted the passionate relationship she was experiencing—the wonderful feeling of being in love that she had never felt before. By doing so, she postponed addressing the deeper, unresolved patterns tied to her pain and sense of self-worth.

3.3.1 The Pivot of Defusion

The central idea of defusion is to help clients recognize that it's not their thoughts that dictate their actions, but rather how they choose to respond to those thoughts. This shift begins when they become aware of the stream of thoughts running through their mind and step back to observe them, instead of automatically believing and acting on them.

A simple yet effective exercise involves saying, "I notice that I am having the thought that…" followed by the specific thought, such as, "I am a worthless person." The goal isn't to determine whether the thought "I am a worthless person" is true or false. Dwelling on such a thought is simply not a helpful way to empower oneself. Learning to see thoughts as just one possible perspective—rather than as an absolute truth—is an unusual skill that many people need to consciously practice. For example, instead of giving in to a self-critical thought, a person might respond, "I notice that I am having the thought that I am a worthless person. Okay, fine. And what am I going to do next?"

Although the principle is straightforward, it requires ongoing practice. Because we are so accustomed to viewing our thoughts as facts, this shift can feel uncomfortable at first. However, the reward for this training is a profound sense of liberation—the freedom to decide what truly matters and to take actions that may not align with preexisting beliefs.

Over time, this approach helps clients reclaim control of their lives, becoming the "boss" of their own choices. It also fosters deeper coherence, as clients begin to live in alignment with their values and prioritize their overall well-being. Ultimately, this leads to a far more fulfilling and authentic way of life.

3.3.2 Defusion and Self-as-Context

Defusion and self-as-context are closely connected. A person's self-image isn't something tangible; it's a network of words and ideas developed over years. This self-image includes simple content like "I am a woman," "I am a father," "I am tall," "I am weak," "I am kind," "I am pretty," as well as more complex rules, such as "When I listen to my friends, I can improve our relationship," "When I am aggressive, I get what I want," "I need to take care of other people's well-being to get attention," and so on. Most of the time, we don't actively question these self-descriptions; we simply live as though they're true. This, in itself, is not a problem, but a natural and efficient part of being human.

We can't constantly ask ourselves in every situation, "Who am I, really?" We need content related to our self to effectively engage in life.

The problem arises when we become stuck—when certain thoughts or rules take on too much significance, dominating other perspectives on ourselves. This makes it very difficult to distance ourselves from these rigid mental patterns, leaving us with only narrow, limited ways of acting, which over time harm our well-being. In other words, we become trapped by our self-content, severely constraining our ability to engage fully in life.

For example, Fanny, who had been terrorized by her father, realized this after her crisis: "I thought I was responsible for my father's well-being. When I distanced myself from him and told him I wouldn't tolerate his anger toward me anymore, I felt like an ice-cold, bad daughter."

Behaving in a new way can feel terrible, even when it aligns with one's values. Fanny's self-image had been shaped by the belief that she was the solely responsible for her father's well-being, as she couldn't rely on her anxious mother as a child. However, through therapy, she began prioritizing her own well-being, disrupting this dysfunctional family dynamic. Predictably, her father resisted these changes and wanted her to return to old patterns.

Fanny had to expand her perspective on herself. She learned to affirm, "It's important to take care of my own well-being and to set boundaries. This will also help me maintain a relationship with my father in the long run." She further practiced telling herself, "I can allow myself to feel 'cold,' but I don't have to buy into it. My father is responsible for his own well-being."

By distancing herself from her difficult thoughts and feelings, Fanny was able to take actions that initially felt wrong but ultimately proved liberating. She learned that prioritizing her own needs didn't make her "bad"—it made her healthier.

The therapeutic goal is to enable new behaviors, because the more options clients have, the better they can adapt their actions to their current situation while moving in valued directions and creating a life they love.

3.4 Acceptance: Yearning to Feel

Another process that is crucial in navigating many uncontrollable life situations is acceptance, and the yearning to feel and to experience (Hayes, 2019). If we look at children, this intuitively makes sense. Children express themselves fully in their unique way. Limits come with language—with learning to label certain experiences as good and desirable, and others as bad and better to avoid.

Fanny's story helps clarify this concept: being yelled at and devalued by her own father was deeply painful for her. When he then claimed to love her despite his harmful behavior, the confusion was profound, causing her to question her own experience—could this treatment really be "loving"? To manage this disconnect, she began ignoring her internal feedback, pushing aside the pain and confusion. While it can be beneficial to occasionally set feelings aside, when it becomes a habitual pattern, it may eventually lead to not feeling much at all. The range of experience narrows on both ends of the spectrum—the painful and the joyful. It's like putting a lid on a vegetable stew: you don't just trap the cabbage you dislike, but also the carrots you'd love to eat.

There are countless ways to disconnect from inner experiences—surfing the internet, drinking alcohol, smoking, overeating, overworking, gaming, watching cat videos, arguing, ruminating, or even exercising or meditating. Anything can become a means of avoidance. When these behaviors are overused, a person may grow numb to the consequences: how tired or uncomfortable the body feels, or even that they're drawn to the wrong people. Their internal warning system gets switched off, creating a vicious cycle.

3.4.1 The Pivot of Acceptance

The pivot of acceptance is helping clients reconnect with their experiences, acknowledging what is present and giving it space. They can then inquire, "What do I need now, and what would be wise and valuable for me to do?"

In therapy, you can guide your clients to tune into their body, identifying areas of tension, pain, or other sensations, and directing them to breathe into the areas that they feel most strongly. By giving space to the tension and observing what unfolds, clients might notice the tension increase, decrease, or transform into something else. The outcome is unpredictable, but the process reestablishes a connection to their internal feedback.

One of my favorite recommendations for clients is to repeat this process for a few breaths or minutes, two or three times a day, asking themselves, "How am I right now? Is there anything that wants to be noticed or taken care of?" Some clients prefer to do it right upon waking up, lying in bed or sitting on the edge of the bed. Others opt for later in the day, perhaps with a cup of tea or coffee during breaks between business meetings. The key is to practice briefly but regularly, making it a habit, like brushing your teeth. It's not necessary to spend too much time on it. On the contrary, that could lead to getting lost and immersed in difficult emotions. Instead, it's better to remain more flexible, turn toward the current feeling for a few breaths, and then return to the task at hand.

In therapy, when painful feelings surface, it's essential to help clients recognize that they are capable of noticing their pain—and strong enough to allow it. They still have the ability to avoid tricky emotions, and when they are in the middle of a business meeting, that might be precisely the right thing to do. You give them back their authority over their feelings. Even if they cannot choose their life story or their feelings, they can practice how much these things should influence their actions today.

Fanny's main avoidance strategy was to keep herself busy in life, rushing through the day, so that she could ignore her difficult feelings. At home, she was used to distracting herself, staying up late, watching TV shows, and only falling asleep with sleeping pills.

Practicing acceptance in session gave her the confidence to apply the exercises at home and to allow herself the feelings of helplessness and hopelessness. It was a tough time for her, and it took several weeks until she reported that her feelings became more bearable and that she had phases of relief. She directly experienced the connection between allowing her painful feelings and the strength and clarity to set boundaries with her father. The longing for the man who had betrayed her disappeared, and she started to experience self-love, joy, and gratitude.

3.4.2 Misunderstandings About Acceptance

Although acceptance—sometimes referred to as willingness—is a key part of psychological flexibility, it is often misunderstood. These misunderstandings can prevent both clients and therapists from engaging with acceptance in a helpful way. Below are some common misconceptions:

- "Accepting means agreeing with what happened." No. Acceptance is not about condoning harmful behaviors such as violence or invalidation. Instead, it's about acknowledging the impact these experiences have had on a person's life. Clients cannot control these effects, but they can learn to respond to them in healthier ways.

- "Accepting means giving up." No. Acceptance is not resignation; it is a conscious, powerful act that often requires great courage. It's like training a new muscle that allows individuals to take meaningful steps forward, even in the face of difficult emotions.
- "If I accept this feeling, it will finally go away." This is a common trap. If your clients say, "I've practiced acceptance every day, but my pain is still there," it likely indicates they are resisting the feeling rather than truly allowing it, leading them to get stuck again.

3.4.3 Acceptance and Self-as-Context

As therapists, we provide our clients with a broader context for the new experience of consciously engaging with their pain. We offer them what was often missing in the original situation: guidance, support, and a safe space to confront their "inner monsters." In this way, we act as their "other-as-context" until they develop their own strength and capacity for self-as-context, which enables them to flexibly connect with their difficult emotions when needed.

With this newfound ability, clients can explore and redefine what is possible for them to do and decide what steps they genuinely want to take. This process is closely tied to their new self-image, as seen in Fanny's case. As long as she clung to the old self-image of being "cool" and "successful," ignoring her vulnerability because the painful experiences felt too overwhelming, she couldn't break free from her damaging relationship with her father.

In a sense, self-as-context implies acceptance on a broader scale. By expanding our inner space, we can embrace everything happening both inside and outside of our bodies. It is a healthy, energy-efficient approach, as resistance and avoidance consume significant energy without actually preventing difficult experiences. Practicing self-as-context allows clients to cultivate aspects of themselves they may never have imagined were possible.

3.5 Presence: Yearning for Orientation

As you might have already suspected, being present is a critical component of growth. You cannot practice acceptance of difficult feelings, distance yourself from your thoughts, or become aware of your self-image without becoming engaged in the present moment.

The yearning behind presence is the desire for orientation (Hayes, 2019). Humans want to know where they are, what is happening around them, and how to make sense of it. This orientation is crucial for both safety and successful survival. However, the human ability to think—while powerful—often interferes by overshadowing sensory perceptions and bodily signals. Unlike other animals, humans are often absent-minded, ruminating about the past ("Why did my partner post that on Instagram? What does it mean?") or worrying about the future ("If she does that again, I'll be so disappointed"). This preoccupation causes us to miss out on information and opportunities in the current moment, such as a colleague's friendly smile or the good smell of the air after rain. It's like walking through a landscape with your nose buried in an ancient map or in future plans, oblivious to the landmarks or even the beauty of your surroundings (Hayes, 2019).

3.5.1 The Pivot of Getting Present

Guiding your clients to mindfully focus on what they are perceiving right here, right now, is the essence of practicing presence. This is what we called self-as-process earlier, e.g., "I experience…" The focus can be narrow or broad ("What do you feel with your fingers" or "What can you perceive with your senses?"), inside or outside the body ("What sensation do you feel inside your body right now?" vs. "What do you hear outside on the street?"), and can be liked or disliked ("Notice if this perception is pleasant or unpleasant for you," "Notice how you evaluate it"). Getting present means "taking the nose out of the map." It enables the person to perceive their surroundings, set a direction, and steer toward it.

The more inflexible a client is—for example, if they avoid contact with you, fail to notice their surroundings, or struggle to name internal experiences—the more simply you need to start, directly in the therapeutic situation.

For instance, in her first session, Fanny talked so much and so quickly that I hardly could get a word in. After listening for a while, noticing my own internal conversation—"I can't work with this person, it's impossible, I'm going crazy"—I kindly asked, "I am sorry to interrupt you, but I am wondering if you are aware of what has been happening in the last twenty minutes." Her immediate response was, "I am talking all the time; I am so nervous." This marked the beginning of our successful collaboration. Together, we looked at the purpose of her constant flow of words, her fear of her feelings, and my potential judgment of her painful story with the man who had treated her badly.

You can incorporate exercises into conversations less formally—rather than saying, "Now we are going to do a mindfulness exercise," you might say:

- "While we're talking, can you feel your feet on the ground?"
- "Notice if it feels easy to allow this experience, or perhaps not so easy."
- "Does this touch on something that is meaningful to you?"

By weaving mindfulness into therapy, you help clients practice being present while simultaneously exploring processes like acceptance and values. This approach helps clients strengthen these essential skills.

For further practice, clients can integrate brief moments of pause into their daily routines. These moments don't need to be elaborate or time-consuming. For example:

- Sitting and feeling their body before getting out of the car
- Taking a few breaths before making a phone call
- Noticing, "These are my children," while playing with them
- Consciously inhaling the fresh air while cycling to work

These practices should be specific, manageable, and enjoyable to foster lasting habits. Such moments of reconnection can be especially valuable during times of high tension. These pauses create opportunities for deliberate decision-making, such as, "I won't take my bad mood out on my partner right now," or, "I will be late. I will let my colleagues know immediately, so they can adjust the meeting agenda." In this way, challenging situations are less likely to escalate unnecessarily, allowing tension to subside more quickly.

3.5.2 Being Present and Self-as-Context

For my clients, I sometimes use the example of a dog. If a dog were sitting here on my sofa, it would feel its bottom touching the seat, smell the air, and see me moving around the room. The dog would be present. But the dog couldn't think or say, "I am sitting here, feeling my bottom touching the seat, smelling the air, and seeing someone moving around."

Humans, however, can do far more than simply feel the sensations of sitting, smelling the air, and seeing someone moving around the room. In addition, we can recognize and label our own feeling, smelling, and seeing—this is what we call self-as-process.

Humans can also become disconnected from their experiences, not noticing their sitting, smelling, and seeing any more—for instance, by getting caught up in ruminations.

On top of that, humans can also observe the "I" that is doing the feeling, smelling, and seeing. We have the ability to notice ourselves from the observer perspective, which we call self-as-context.

When clients become more aware of their inner and outer experiences—such as mental chatter, emotions, bodily sensations, and sensory perceptions—they also begin to notice their automatic reactions to these experiences. For example: "Every time I think about the exam, I start sweating and stop studying," or "Whenever I smell this fragrance, I feel the urge to eat something."

Awareness of these connections between experiences and reactions creates a beneficial distance, deeper insights, and the possibility for alternative responses. A client can experiment with more diverse and healthier reactions, such as: "If I feel anxious about the exam, I'll call my friend for reassurance that I can handle it," or "Instead of eating when I smell this fragrance, I'll start dancing." This process helps clients expand their sense of self and explore new ways of being.

3.6 Values: Yearning for Meaning and Self-Direction

When your clients develop more presence and a more flexible sense of self, their ability to notice what truly matters to them also increases. LeJeune and Luoma (2019) describe values as ongoing behaviors, freely chosen life directions that we actively want to translate into actions. Values inspire us and touch our hearts. Just because they are freely chosen does not mean they are arbitrary. Like all our behaviors, they are influenced by our learning history, biology, culture, social circumstances, and other factors. As therapists, we help our clients explore the diversity of available values and identify those they consider important, both now and in the long term. Additionally, we also support them in finding actions to express those values (LeJeune & Luoma, 2019).

The yearning behind values is the longing for meaning and purpose in our lives. For centuries, humans have grappled with questions like, "Why am I alive? What is the purpose of life?" ACT originator Steven Hayes states, "There is no yearning more important to human beings than to freely pick and pursue their life direction" (2019, p. 224).

Seeing oneself as superior to others, being self-righteous, basing one's actions on social expectations and others' approval, or prioritizing possessions, fame, and power over relationships can be distorted ways of seeking meaning in life.

Our purpose is not given to us—it is something we choose, granting us the freedom to shape our own lives. A valued direction serves as a guiding force for our actions and decisions, much like a magnet aligning iron filings, helping to bring our behaviors into alignment.

3.6.1 The Pivot of Valuing

Exploring values in therapy is often an inspiring and profoundly moving process. The turning point toward uncovering values can emerge from different perspectives. You can simply ask your clients, "What is so valuable to you that you have come to therapy?" or, "What is important to you in this area of your life?" You can help them notice that a particular action or experience resonates with them and conclude that it holds value: "I was thrilled when I received the news that I could do an externship as a teacher in another country. I never realized how valuable it is for me to connect with different cultures."

Values can also emerge from painful experiences, as a result of asking questions like, "This experience is so painful for you—there must be something here that matters deeply to you; if there wasn't, it wouldn't be so distressing. What could that value be?" Clients often find relief when they examine the value behind the pain and realize that where they care most, they are also most vulnerable.

Other helpful shifts in perspective include "Imagine looking at this situation in thirty years—from the perspective of your older self, what would be a good decision, and what would you be proud of?" and "Imagine celebrating your seventieth birthday with friends and family, and someone is giving a speech about what makes you so special and what others can count on in you—what would you most like to hear?"

Valuing is a conscious behavior and an ongoing process, requiring awareness and practice. Acting according to our values is not necessarily pleasant, and can even be challenging, requiring courage, persistence, and discipline. Sometimes no one else is watching, and we do not receive applause. Sometimes it can be expensive, for example when you pay taxes honestly, because you value integrity. Staying committed to our values might sometimes feel like a sacrifice, but in the long run, it empowers us, as we stay true to ourselves.

Fanny became aware of her values through a painful therapeutic process. Before that, she sometimes felt that something was missing but couldn't quite pinpoint what it was. She believed her values were rooted in working hard and being successful, unaware that this was actually an avoidance strategy that came at the cost of her well-being. As she reflected more deeply on her harmful relationships with her father and her former partner, she realized how important it was for her to be able to openly express her desires and feel heard. She wanted to find a kind partner and a relationship where she and her partner would mutually respect each other's boundaries.

This realization was a profound lesson learned from her painful experiences, giving her a deep sense of peace. Whenever she fell back into old patterns, she eventually noticed it and redirected her attention to her values. There is something wonderful about values: they are always available, and you can pivot back to them at any time.

3.6.2 Some Traps Around Values

Values can bring clarity on what truly matters and inspire new actions. However, to ensure they serve their intended purpose, it's important to be aware of several common pitfalls that can undermine their effectiveness:

1. Presuming what should be valuable for our clients: As therapists, we cannot know what is valuable to our clients. Our role is to create space for them to discover that for themselves.
2. Becoming rigid or self-righteous about values: For example, "My partner is not doing it right. He should know that this is important to me." Values are a personal choice, and imposing them on others will not lead to a positive outcome.
3. Using values to devalue oneself: Clients might use their values to criticize themselves, such as by saying, "I am a loving person—and I hate myself when I'm not loving!" In these cases, values become integrated into old behavioral patterns (e.g., "not being good enough").
4. Confusing values with materialistic goals or achievements: For example, "My value is to earn a lot of money" or "I want to be famous." A helpful approach is to explore the value behind the goal: "If you had a lot of money, what about that would be valuable to you?"

3.6.3 Values and Self-as-Context

We've already noted that clients need self-as-context skills to become aware of their values. Recognizing one's values requires self-awareness—the ability to notice one's actions, thoughts, and feelings. It also demands a broader perspective from which clients can view their actions and experiences, looking at themselves in the past, present, and future. This broader perspective creates more space, fosters deeper connection with oneself, and brings greater clarity around priorities.

A value is never the "right" perspective; it is simply one meaningful possibility among many. Values are not meant to become rules or standards of perfectionism. From the overarching self-as-context perspective, you help clients gently acknowledge their strengths and limitations in a given situation, and to then consider the next step that aligns with their values. When there is a gap between a person's action and their values, it does not mean failure—it means the value matters.

It is helpful to develop new structures with clients that help them stay aligned with their values. This could include keeping a values journal, making an agreement with a partner about which values they want to focus in the near future, or creating a visual display to track values-based actions.

As a therapist, you are modeling valued behavior for your clients, so keeping your own values in focus will serve as a source of strength and guidance. With this foundation, there's no need to blame either a client or yourself in challenging situations—for example, when a client repeatedly attends sessions without following through on their plans. In such moments, you can assess whether your collaboration has been valuable for them so far: Are they acting more in line with their values? What barriers still remain? You can explore new ideas together and even acknowledge when you feel at a loss with your expertise.

3.7 Committed Action: Yearning for Competence

"There is no 'value' in the absence of action" (LeJeune & Luoma, 2019, p. 11). While recognizing our inherent self-worth—regardless of our actions or achievements—is often an important first step, values without corresponding actions will not bring lasting fulfillment. Lying on the sofa, thinking, "I really care about having good friends," will not be satisfying in the long run if we don't spend time with them.

In ACT, actions that are aligned with values are referred to as "committed actions." In this domain, we yearn for competence (Hayes, 2019), which we cannot experience in inaction. From an early age, we want to participate, move something, make an impact, all of which give us a deep sense of satisfaction, as you probably recognize from when you have overcome your own challenges. The rigid versions of this yearning are overworking and procrastination (or a combination of both), primarily driven by perfectionism and the fear of failure (Hayes, 2019).

Giving clients more freedom to change their behavior is the ultimate goal of all therapeutic approaches. Behavioral activation—doing things that are important to the person, or at least were important to them before they became depressed, anxious, etc.—is one of the best-established therapeutic interventions in terms of its effectiveness. Clients often say things like, "Yes, I would really like to see my friends more, but I can't, I'm too depressed." As a therapist, you know that this is a trap. It's the other way around: when clients begin to take action on things that are important to them, their well-being will improve (Wersebe et al., 2017).

3.7.1 The Pivot of Commitment

The turning point in the area of commitment is to help your clients act purposefully and in alignment with their values in a given situation (Hayes, 2019). Clients often express that following through on a commitment requires courage, because it challenges their existing self-as-content and pushes them to expand their view of themselves—a step that is valuable and healing in itself.

Values serve as a source of strength, providing a pull toward a desired direction. This can help establish new behaviors in a way that feels less like being pushed (e.g., "This will be better for your health in the long run" or "Studies show that overcoming anxiety requires confronting it"), which often activates resistance. Instead, a valued action like "Being free to visit my beloved grandchildren overseas by overcoming my fear of flying" is likely to be far more motivating.

Fanny exemplified committed action in several ways. For instance, she allowed herself to be vulnerable and feel her pain, and she expanded her social connections despite the "waves of pain" washing over her. She stood up to her father, telling him she would no longer listen to him when he yelled at her. And in a new relationship, she openly expressed her desires and boundaries, despite being terribly afraid that her partner would react without understanding and that she would lose the relationship again.

For Fanny, engaging in her values led to some challenging months. The rewards of her courage were not immediate, though she often felt relief once a wave of pain had passed. Her longing to feel alive—to feel not just the pain but also joy—gave her the strength to persevere. When she began to experience inner peace and freedom, she knew she was on the right path. Expanding her social connections and sharing her struggles with friends helped her stabilize and regain her foundation.

With her father, the result was a sense of greater freedom. His behavior improved temporarily but eventually returned to yelling, prompting her to hang up the phone again. She came to accept that his behavior was outside her control, choosing instead to maintain contact with him on her own terms.

Sometimes clients may become fixated on the outcome of their committed actions. At times, the results will align with their hopes; other times, things may turn out differently. This is an important point to evaluate during sessions. Did the committed step bring the client closer to their desired direction? If yes, they can continue practicing the new behavior. If not, what did they learn? What didn't work? What can they adjust or do differently next time? It's also important for clients to recognize that some outcomes are beyond their control. Flexibility enables clients to discern whether it's time to double down on their efforts, or whether acceptance would be more useful. Flexibility also involves exploring different committed actions, all leading toward the same meaningful direction.

Metaphors can help clients avoid getting stuck, such as: "Remember when your children were learning to walk? How often they fell and got back up again?" or "You play the violin—did it sound great the first time you tried?"

The benefits of committed actions are significant. Taking new steps, chosen from a broader perspective, often leads to new experiences of the self. It fosters a sense of self-efficacy, as clients actively shape their lives in a self-chosen direction.

3.7.2 Commitment Requires Self-as-Context

It is essential for clients to consciously connect their actions with their values. This connection doesn't happen automatically—it's a mindful effort that requires a broader perspective on oneself. For example, in the morning, when a client feels annoyed about having to go to work, they can remind themself that they're doing it because it contributes to something meaningful, for example providing for their family. This perspective transforms the action from something they "have to do" into something they choose to do because it matters to them. While the outward behavior—getting up and going to work—remains the same, the inner experience may shift. By aligning their actions with their values, clients expand their perspectives and gain both short-term empowerment, by overcoming barriers, and long-term fulfillment, through living a self-determined life.

Living in accordance with their values often benefits the client's social environment. Values in the sense we use it here aren't pursued solely for oneself. For instance, if someone values respect, their behavior will naturally reflect that in their interactions with others.

To turn valued actions into reality, clients will need all six core change processes mentioned earlier. They'll need:

- Self-as-context: To create space for all experiences—including their inner struggles—gain distance from it, and integrate it as a part of their unique, multifaceted humanity.
- Defusion: To manage the internal voices that scream, "Don't do this—it's dangerous and will end in disaster."
- Acceptance: To allow the difficult emotions that arise when they dare to try something new.

- Presence: To stay connected with the ongoing process, noticing thoughts, feelings, and actions—and recognizing that, in most cases, no one is in mortal danger.
- Values: To reconnect with what truly matters and identify meaningful goals and directions.
- Committed action: To take consistent, purposeful steps aligned with their values.

By practicing these processes, clients can act with purpose and integrity, creating meaningful and lasting change in their lives.

3.8 Summary

An advanced ACT model identifies the deep-seated yearnings or intrinsic motivations underlying each of the six psychological flexibility processes. It suggests that clinical symptoms arise when these yearnings are pursued in a rigid or distorted manner. However, it also emphasizes that you can shift your perspective and actions at any time toward a healthier, more values-oriented direction (Hayes, 2019).

The Pivot of Self-as-Context

The pivotal step toward a more flexible and fulfilling life in the realm of self involves guiding clients to adopt a broader perspective of themselves as whole, multifaceted individuals—embracing all of their aspects, including their flaws, strengths, and vulnerabilities. This process demands courage and practice, as it involves confronting long-avoided pain—such as not receiving the love, acceptance, and safe space they needed, or feeling rejected, flawed, and wronged. When a rigid self-image begins to crumble, it can feel destabilizing and even threatening, which is why it's crucial to let clients control the pace of this work.

The pivot toward self-as-context encourages clients to remain present with themselves, to better understand their challenges, to practice self-compassion, and to recognize their deeper yearnings. As a therapist, your presence creates a safe and supportive space for clients to take these transformative steps. You also serve as a model for them, showing them how they can approach others.

Defusion and Self-as-Context

Defusion and self-as-context are interconnected. Defusion involves stepping back from words, rules, and associated emotions that limit flexible action and are part of the clients' self-content (e.g., "I am weak," "I am suffering," "When I am generous, my friends will like me better," "When I am nice, I get what I want"). Self-as-context, on the other hand, refers to distancing yourself from the narrative that has developed over the years from such thoughts—what becomes "the truth about yourself," "your nature," or what we refer to as "self-as-content."

Practicing defusion and self-as-context means undermining this inflexibility on different levels and helping your clients find a new, expanded relationship to their self-as-content, thereby cultivating new aspects of their self.

Acceptance and Self-as-Context

By practicing acceptance as a therapist, you provide your clients with a broader context for engaging with their pain. You offer them what was often missing in the original situation: guidance, support, and the safety they need to face their inner turmoil. In this role, we act as their "other-as-context" for a time, supporting them until they develop their own strength and capacity for self-as-context. This empowers them to connect with their difficult emotions in a more flexible and constructive way when needed.

In essence, self-as-context involves acceptance on a much larger scale.

Being Present and Self-as-Context

When you're present, you are aware of your experiences. You can notice and name your own feeling, thinking, smelling, seeing, and acting—which is what we call self-as-process.

Beyond that, you can also observe that "I-here-now" is the one noticing and naming the feeling, thinking, smelling, seeing, and acting. This broader perspective is what we call self-as-context.

Working on becoming more aware of inner and outer experiences also means noticing automatic reactions to these experiences (e.g., "Every time I think about the exam, I start sweating and stop studying."). This awareness helps to create a sense of distance and the possibility for alternative, healthier responses, to expand the sense of self.

Values and Self-as-Context

Self-as-context skills are essential for recognizing your values. Adopting an overarching perspective allows you to observe your actions and experiences across time—past, present, and future. This expanded view creates more inner space, deepens your connection with yourself, and brings greater clarity about your priorities. When clients connect with their values, they gain an internal navigation system to guide their actions.

Commitment Requires Self-as-Context

It is essential for clients to consciously connect their actions to their values. This connection doesn't happen automatically—it requires intentional effort (e.g., "I want to provide for my family, so I go to work" versus "I have to go to work"). By aligning their actions with their values, clients shift their perspective from focusing on momentary obstacles to following a longer-term direction. This alignment offers both short-term empowerment, through overcoming immediate barriers, and long-term fulfillment, through living a self-determined, values-driven life.

Step back from yourself, slip out of the thought machine.

No problem you must solve awaits an immediate solution.

Here and now, all is well with you in me.

—Nils, forty-five years old, librarian

CHAPTER 4

When Cues Are Missing: Effects on the Development of Self

Having a diverse and flexible repertoire of actions is advantageous when facing challenging situations and difficult emotions. At its core, the question is: Can we access and utilize our experiences and self-knowledge to act in fulfilling and meaningful ways? Or are we driven by our urges and impulses, leading to ineffective actions that conflict with our deeper values?

In this chapter, we will explore how various experiences influence a child's development, and how those experiences impact the different aspects of the self as the child grows into adulthood:

- Self-as-process: What does it mean when someone struggles to recognize and name their ongoing stream of thoughts, emotions, and bodily sensations?
- Self-as-content: What happens when a person becomes overly fused with their story about themselves?
- Self-as-context: What are the implications when someone struggles to adopt a more distant perspective on themself or others?

These three self-processes are complex verbal skills, and we are far from fully understanding everything about their development—including how they interact with each other, or with genetics, epigenetics, culture, preverbal experiences, and more. However, by studying the connections between how children learn and the dominance of certain patterns, we can identify effective and impactful interventions.

In practice, this complexity can show up in deeply human ways—for example when young parents feel anxious or guilty about doing something wrong because their child doesn't develop according to the norms. Every child is different and responds uniquely to a parent's cues. If you work with parents—or are a parent—it is not about getting everything right. Blame is rarely a useful perspective. What's more helpful is to curiously observe the interplay between your child's behavior and your own, and to adjust step by step in response to the specific situation.

4.1 Cues Are Key

We need language to develop a sense of self. Private experiences—such as thoughts, emotions, and body sensations—play a crucial role in shaping our identity. This is especially true for internal self-descriptions, such as "I am an optimistic person," "I am persistent," or "I am boring." These self-statements are invisible to others, yet our actions may offer clues about them. Simultaneously, however, when a person opens up, we are often surprised by how their self-image differs from the impression we have of them.

People often become aware of their self-content or develop new aspects of it through verbal expression. For example, if someone says, "You are working really hard on this," the individual might reflect and realize, "Yes, I think I am a persistent person." This can even lead to a new insight: "I never realized how persistent I can be." In this way, new self-content is formed and added to a person's self-story. Throughout life, this network of self-stories continues to evolve. New self-content can be acquired, and certain aspects of the self may become more prominent during specific life stages (e.g., valuing hard work when starting a career), while others, such as playfulness, may fade into the background.

Returning to the origins of language learning in childhood, developing a rich inner life and the ability to accurately identify internal experiences requires countless examples and consistent reinforcement. When caregivers respond attentively to their toddler's signals—such as by recognizing whether they are seeking food, physical contact, or expressing anger or joy—they reinforce "a broad range of signaling behaviors" (Whittingham, 2014, p. 213). In other words, they then encourage their infant to display multifaceted behaviors.

As children grow, parents continue to observe signs of internal states—like a smile or tears—and assign meaning to these expressions. In this way, they support the child in building a framework for understanding their inner world. For example, asking questions like "Do you like this cake?" or "Are you sad because Grandma is leaving?" helps the child connect physical sensations (like chest tightness or tears) to specific emotions (like sadness) and contexts (like Grandma leaving). Parents who acknowledge a wide range of their child's physical and emotional self-expression—offering loving attention and clear guidance when necessary—help their child develop a rich variety of self-expression and a nuanced understanding of their own inner world.

4.1.1 Lack of Cues

When external cues are rare or inaccurate, it becomes more challenging for the child to learn to accurately identify and articulate their inner experiences. Children need emotional talk, and when caregivers avoid discussing their feelings or attempt to hide their emotions, children miss out on critical opportunities to learn how external events relate to internal emotional states. For example, when parents argue and the mother cries because she is sad, a child at a certain developmental stage will intuitively link these two events. However, if the mother denies her sadness and says, "I'm not sad; I'm crying because something flew into my eye," the child becomes confused and misses the chance to learn the connection between conflict and sadness.

A lack of emotional cues can also occur when caregivers ignore or fail to acknowledge or name their child's expressions of emotion, such as facial expressions, body language, or other signals. This might happen, for example, when a caregiver dismisses the child's distress by saying, "You're fine; nothing happened," instead of validating the child's pain and offering comfort. Such responses deprive the child of a framework to interpret and process their emotions.

Another scenario is when parents ask children to hug a relative they dislike or do not know, in order to conform to social norms. The child then receives contradictory information: their inner feelings ("dislike") versus external expectations ("act as if you like the person"). This discrepancy might teach the child to ignore their internal feedback over time, as the mismatch feels uncomfortable. Alternatively, if the child resists the hug and is then reprimanded, they may become reluctant to trust their inner guidance in the future.

Parents might also provide socially acceptable but inaccurate interpretations of the child's emotions. For instance, when the child expresses aversion, a parent might say, "Are you anxious about your aunt?" Such comments could lead the child to misinterpret their feelings of aversion as anxiety, potentially causing them to see themselves as an "anxious child." Over time, the child may begin interpreting neutral signals, such as a pounding heart after running, as signs of anxiety. This cycle can entrench the child in rigid self-perceptions (Feldman Barrett, 2017; McHugh et al., 2019).

Caregivers may have various reasons for not being attentive to their children's inner lives. They might be overwhelmed by their own struggles, lack emotional awareness due to their own upbringing, or worry that focusing too much on emotions will make their child overly sensitive.

For a child, the absence of acknowledgment can be deeply painful. Their internal experiences are vivid, yet they receive too little guidance to interpret them and do not experience the relief that comes from being understood. You may hear clients say things like, "Nobody cared about how I was feeling or what I wanted," or "My parents didn't really listen to me; they were so busy." These statements often hint at a lack of emotional cues during critical developmental stages.

4.1.2 Rigid Cues

Research suggests that parents' ability to engage in flexible behavior significantly influences a child's capacity to develop flexible behaviors and, consequently, a flexible sense of self. When parents consistently display the same type of response regardless of the child's signals (e.g., being controlling, demanding, cold, or overly enthusiastic), the child may struggle to develop a nuanced range of behaviors, which can negatively impact their emotional regulation, social interactions, and psychological adaptability. As psychologist Whittingham (2014) noted, "Sensitive caregiving is not merely warm and loving; it is sensitively timed to the infant's signals" (p. 213).

Parents who experience high levels of stress and low psychological flexibility often respond unfavorably to their children's behavior, perceiving their children as difficult. This perception can lead to feelings of helplessness, resulting in even more rigid parenting responses, which in turn further escalates the child's challenging behavior and the parent's distress. Parental stress has also been linked to maladjustment in children, manifesting in restlessness, overactivity, heightened fearfulness, difficulties with peers, and lower social competence (Fonseca, Moreira, & Canavarro, 2020; Flujas-Contreras et al., 2023).

Similarly, McHugh et al. (2019) suggest that children raised by parents who are perceived as frequently annoyed or overly dominant may develop a rigid sense of self. Such children are more likely to prioritize pleasing others over attending to their own experiences, becoming driven by compliance rather than intrinsic motivation. This pattern can limit their ability to explore their own individuality and may hinder their emotional and social well-being.

Rigid parenting behavior can take various forms, including:

- Being intrusive and overly demanding
- Restricting the child's exploration through excessive control
- Being cold and displaying low levels of responsiveness

- Providing inconsistent or unclear rules
- Excessively praising and overvaluing the child's actions, regardless of the significance of the achievement
- Attributing the child's difficulties solely to the child or exclusively to external factors

Parenting is a complex challenge, and parents who experience high levels of distress and low psychological flexibility often require support. It is unfortunate when such parents cannot enjoy time with their children, and instead develop negative thoughts and feelings toward themselves and their children. Learning psychological flexibility skills would benefit both parents and children, promoting healthier family dynamics and greater enjoyment of their relationships.

Naturally, every child's self-development is shaped by their caregivers. As therapists, it is crucial for us to assess whether a client's ability to act effectively has been impaired and whether their difficulty in recognizing and articulating their inner world contributes to this challenge.

4.1.3 Invalidating or Hostile Cues

The development of the self is especially harmed when caregivers are covertly or openly hostile or neglectful. This includes situations where children experience verbal or physical violence against themselves or close others, or grow up in a threatening environment where they are humiliated and devalued as a person (Schiraldi, 2021; McHugh & Stapleton, 2021). It is almost unbearable for a child to endure constant hostile feedback or no attention at all. Renowned psychologist Hayes (2019, p. 193) poignantly states, "The single hardest burden for a human being to carry is a lack of nurturance in childhood."

In many such families, parents struggle with their own mental health, suffering for example from severe forms of addiction, schizophrenia, or depression. In such environments, a child might have to take care of themself early on, often taking on responsibilities for their siblings and even parents, while receiving little to no parental care. These difficult circumstances and challenging life experiences can have a lasting impact on the child's development, affecting not only their sense of self but also physical factors like hormones, immune systems, epigenetics, and neurological development—effects that can persist well into adulthood (Schiraldi, 2021).

A child in their early years of language acquisition has no concept of others' perspectives; they relate all experiences to themself. Even as they grow older, distancing themself from neglectful or abusive parents remains challenging, because it's difficult for a child to think, "This is my parents' failure; it says nothing about me." As a result, neglect or abuse often teach the child harmful lessons about themself, such as believing they are unworthy of kindness and care.

After repeated disappointing interactions, a child may develop distorted methods of seeking attention, often by displaying rigid behaviors. Among other possibilities, these behaviors can manifest as excessive politeness, ambition, rudeness, aggression, or withdrawal. The crucial point is that the behavioral repertoire becomes narrow and repetitive, offering few choices for the child, a condition that often persists into adulthood.

These descriptions are not meant to blame caregivers or a difficult childhood for current behavior. That would only result in clients being stuck in the past and unable to take responsibility for their lives now. Instead, it's about recognizing potential influencing factors, so that clients can develop understanding and self-compassion for their own unhelpful behavior. Together, you and your client can then identify points of intervention.

It's important to note that the necessary skills can be learned at any age; clients just need the guidance that was lacking in earlier years.

4.2 Impact on Self-as-Process Skills

If a child is not stimulated by their caregivers' interest, questions, and guidance, they may struggle to develop an interest in their own inner life. As Skinner (1976) observes, "It is only when a person's private world becomes important to others that it is made important to him" (S. 35). Without this external validation, the child may tend to ignore or misinterpret their inner experiences.

A central aspect of self-as-process is its role in fostering self-efficacy. Skinner refers to this as "self-knowledge," which provides the person with "a better position to predict and control his own behavior" (1976, S. 35). For example, when a child is sad, they may cry and eventually be comforted. Self-knowledge, however, arises when parents show interest by naming the experience—saying, "Oh, you're sad"—allowing the child to connect the perception in the body with the corresponding word and the relief that follows being solaced. This knowledge gives a person much more control over their responses and needs.

Especially in the realm of emotions, knowing your emotions, recognizing their triggers, and identifying helpful responses are all vital strengths. A lack of skills in these areas can lead to various challenges, impacting emotional regulation and decision-making.

4.2.1 Missing Labels for Emotions

Emotions are closely related to both the body and language. Through language, we learn to associate bodily states (e.g., "butterflies in my stomach") with emotional concepts (e.g., "joy"). Emotions play a vital role in guiding us—revealing what we like or dislike, and alerting us when something feels wrong. According to Feldman Barrett (2017), emotions serve several important functions:

1. EMOTIONS CREATE MEANING

Emotions help us interpret our private experiences within a context, providing explanations for our states. For instance:

- "Is my heart pounding because I'm in love or because I climbed a steep hill?"
- "Is my stomach tightening because I'm anxious about an exam or because I've eaten something spoiled?"

2. EMOTIONS GUIDE OUR ACTIONS

Emotions offer essential cues for decision-making and action, such as:

- "I think I want to meet this person again."
- "I went too fast, so I'll slow down."

- "I'd better start studying for the exam."
- "I need to seek medical attention."

3. EMOTIONS HELP REGULATE OUR BODY'S ENERGY BUDGET

Emotions are tied to physical responses that help maintain balance. For example, a child feeling anxious may seek close body contact with a safe caregiver, which soothes their arousal. Emotions activate bodily responses based on our interpretations, such as relaxation, muscle tension, increased energy when needed, or the release of cortisol during fear, all of which help manage the body's energy and stress levels.

4. EMOTIONS SERVE A SOCIAL FUNCTION

Emotions enable us to connect with others by helping us recognize when someone needs comfort or when to share in their joy. They allow us to anticipate behavior; for example, if someone appears furious, we may avoid confrontation. Within a culture, societies agree on emotional concepts to facilitate community living. If someone is unfamiliar with key emotional concepts, they are excluded from a vital aspect of social interaction, making it challenging to integrate into social groups, as emotions play a central role in mutual understanding.

When people lack clear emotional labels—especially for difficult emotions that remain nonverbal, vague, and often show up as unpleasant bodily experiences—it becomes harder for them to interpret their internal experiences, respond effectively, and connect with others. Understanding the different functions of emotions illustrates why bringing emotions into verbal awareness and having a rich emotional vocabulary matters.

4.2.2 Emotional Avoidance

A central issue in nearly all types of psychological problems is emotional avoidance (Törneke, 2010). Without adequate practice and guidance, emotions can feel like threatening monsters, especially because of their related physical sensations, which are rooted in the body through hormonal responses and neuronal activity long before we acquire language. Through language, we gain a deeper understanding and differentiation of these physical sensations and learn how to deal with them. We learn that, for example, "this feeling in the belly is called fear," what "fear" even means, that others also experience it, when it typically arises, and what one can do about it.

Without this understanding, emotions can feel like they strike out of nowhere, appearing massive and overwhelming, leaving us feeling powerless to stop them. The threat feels real, as we truly experience emotions physically, and so the meaning we assign to them also seems true—for example, "I'm terribly scared; this must be very dangerous!"

Even animals instinctively avoid unpleasant experiences when possible. Similarly, it's intuitive—especially for someone who lacks emotional regulation skills—to avoid emotions. People often numb themselves through excessive food, alcohol, overpacked schedules, extreme physical activity, or by chasing intense pleasurable emotions via substance use, gaming, shopping, or other distractions. Additionally, rumination is another common but maladaptive strategy for avoiding emotions.

These avoidance strategies may provide short-term relief, but they disconnect individuals from a vital part of their being. Although painful emotions might subside temporarily, overall suffering tends to deepen over time.

Avoidance can lead to a negative cycle. By not engaging with emotions, individuals miss the opportunity to increase their self-awareness, such as, "When I'm scared, it helps to check whether there's a real threat. If there isn't one, I can calm myself by going for a walk." Over time, a disconnect can result in losing access to one's emotional feedback system almost entirely (McHugh and Stapleton, 2021). In all cases of emotional avoidance, the dynamic exchange between the inner and outer worlds becomes stifled. This restriction fosters unfortunate cycles that reinforce outdated and unhelpful self-stories, perpetuating distress and suffering.

But feelings or emotions (I use these terms interchangeably, with a preference for "emotions" when referring to more intense or accumulated feelings) cannot simply be erased; they are behavioral patterns embedded in our bodily systems. When a triggering event occurs, the emotion is activated. To illustrate this, I often use the metaphor of an ice canal: once you are set in motion, you must follow the canal to its end—there is no way out along the way. The most painful emotions are often the most persistent because they once played a crucial role in survival.

Another metaphor I share with clients is that ignored emotions can behave like little children seeking attention—they become louder and more insistent until they are finally acknowledged. Emotions have a purpose: they exist to protect you. They are not your enemy but are here to serve you.

The good news is that you can make peace with overwhelming emotions at any time. Listening to them, rather than avoiding them, leads to long-term relief. This approach allows you to uncover your true needs and longings, enabling you to take much better care of yourself.

4.2.3 Losing the Internal Compass

When the emotional feedback system is disrupted, the internal compass is thrown off course. Listening to our emotions means slowing down, reflecting on their message, and deciding whether to follow their guidance. However, when this feedback system is unavailable—when one's internal world feels numb, or when perception is limited to a narrow range of emotions—decision-making becomes much more difficult.

In such cases, a child often turns to external sources for orientation. They become highly skilled at figuring out what their caregivers need. Alternatively, they might rely on rules they have learned are effective, such as "When Mom and Dad are fighting, it's better to hide in my room" or "When Mom looks tired, I try to help her." By doing so, they can avoid punishment or perhaps at least gain some attention.

This reliance on external orientation becomes even more significant as perspective-taking abilities develop—a topic we will explore further in the section on self-as-context.

4.3 Impact on Self-as-Content

Scientific research has shown that our capacity for language can increase our suffering in already painful situations. Many of the symptoms you observe in your clinical practice can be traced back to our language abilities. For example, our pain is often amplified by our need for coherence ("Why do I keep ending up in the same harmful relationships?"), our tendency to accept words or feelings as the truth ("I am a loser. This is how it is."), and our inclination to simplify life through rigid rules ("It's better to never have an intimate relationship again than to suffer like this.").

Furthermore, in every language community, there are societal expectations regarding roles (e.g., how you should be as a mother, father, student, elder, etc.), rules (e.g., "When you're not happy, something is wrong with you"), labels, and ideals (often formed through comparison to others) (McHugh et al., 2019). We absorb these beliefs by learning language, watching movies, reading novels, engaging with social media, and conversing with others. However, we can only observe others from the outside; we cannot see what is happening within them. This creates a distorted picture, because we compare our inner selves to the external appearances of others and often conclude that others are doing better.

These individual and societal influences contribute significantly to our self-content. While these influences can teach us navigate the complexities of life, they—once again—can hinder our connection to our vital internal feedback system.

The aforementioned factors are discussed in more detail as follows. They are not clearly delineated from one another, but instead overlap and reinforce each other.

4.3.1 Coherence and Literality: Repeating the Same Old Story

Perhaps you know the feeling when you're working on a puzzle and finally find the piece that fits perfectly into the gap—"Yes!" Our minds work similarly: they seek out pieces that fit with what they already know, often overlooking those that don't fit into the picture. In fact, our minds can even convince us that a piece fits perfectly when, in reality, it doesn't.

We call this phenomenon "coherence," which refers to "the situation when the parts of something fit together in a natural or reasonable way" (Villatte, 2024). The phenomenon of coherence is well researched and deeply embedded in language learning (Törneke, 2010). When a child learns language, for example, "this is a tree" translates to "this word is the same as a tree." No one says, "It's arbitrary, we could call it anything, and the word is not the same as the thing." No—it is a tree, and that is the "right" word! We are heavily reinforced for using the "right" words, first by our proud parents and later by our community, with all the advantages of sharing the same language: understanding each other, participating, collaborating, and predicting the behavior of others.

Coherence becomes self-reinforcing, and this applies to our self-image as well. While coherence is helpful in many ways, it can also be at the root of unhealthy behavior. Since we experience incoherence as unpleasant or punishing, we automatically strive to create and maintain a coherent picture of ourselves, even to our own detriment (Villatte et al., 2015). For example, if a person has the self-concept that they are despicable, they may unconsciously gravitate toward people who confirm that belief, while overlooking friendly signals from others who genuinely like them.

Perception is shaped by previous experiences, and we tend to notice more of what fits into our existing framework. It feels easier and safer to navigate a familiar environment, both internally and externally, than to risk encountering something new.

Additionally, it feels good to be right. We all know the satisfaction of saying, "Yes! I knew it would go this way!" Even when things go wrong, we can find some form of satisfaction in being "right." In some situations, this might be the only form of distorted "control" we can achieve—the feeling that we "knew it all along."

Literality—the extent to which we believe our verbal descriptions about ourselves or anything else are the truth—amplifies the effect of coherence, as we begin to see our beliefs as the absolute truth, rather than just one possible perspective (McHugh, et al., 2019). For instance, if a client has been deceived and states that their "trust in their partner is forever shattered," for them, this is the truth, not just one possible perspective or choice. They will adjust their behavior to fit this perspective and suffer as a result, yet see no way out because "that's just how it is."

4.3.2 Self-Labeling and Self-Rules

Related to coherence and literality is the issue of self-labels and self-rules, which also emerge through language. A rule, or a self-rule when applied to the self, anticipates which behavior leads to which consequence—for example, "When I care for others, I will grab their attention" (Törneke, 2010).

Parents naturally care for their offspring, so when they don't, a child must find a way to cope with the absence of that care. As soon as a child learns language, they will try to make sense of being neglected, and the mind constructs a story to explain why they didn't receive the care they needed. Oftentimes, the explanation will lean toward self-blame, leading the child to believe they are undeserving of love and support, and that any neglect was their own fault. A thought might arise, such as "There must be something wrong with me, otherwise this wouldn't happen to me," which is an example of a self-rule. The self-label might then become "I am worthless."

Neglect by parents is unfathomable for a child. In their small world, where they see themself as the center, they can only conclude that the fault lies within themself, especially when they have not yet developed the perspective-taking capacities to discriminate their own behavior from their parents' behavior. Even if the child senses that the parents' behavior is wrong, they still love their caregivers. They are dependent on them and may grapple with a persistent loyalty conflict, not wanting to blame their parents.

Moreover, it is preferable to have some control through the thought, "It's my own fault; I could have done something differently," than to feel completely helpless in the face of parental neglect. As the child grows older and begins to understand their parents' wrongdoing, the seeds of self-doubt, guilt, and self-devaluation have already been planted.

The more threatening the world is for a child—such as through sexual, physical, and emotional abuse, or neglect, being invalidated, and being ignored—the less control the child has in the external world. In response, the child seeks some kind of control in their internal world, often through explanations like "I must be disgusting because my mother told me she wished I had never been born." A related self-rule could be "I am disgusting, and that's why others don't like me. To avoid being disappointed again, I keep my distance from others."

Naturally, no child consciously decides, "What rules do I want to establish and follow?" Instead, rules develop intuitively with language and behavior, shaped and refined over time—often without much conscious awareness—based on how adaptive they are in the child's context and how well they support survival. Structuring behavior through rules is an efficient way to navigate the world; we do it all the time, as in, "When it's cold, I better wear a sweater." It's only problematic when we become insensitive to the present environment and continue to follow outdated or harmful rules, even when our circumstances have changed.

From the perspective of acceptance and commitment therapy, the root of suffering in painful situations lies not in the content of the labels and rules, but in relating to them as though they were true. In other words, the suffering arises from the client's fusion with their thoughts and the resulting narrowed perception, which can limit their ability to interact with the present environment and prevent new experiences from occurring (McHugh et al., 2019; Törneke, 2010).

4.3.3 Insensitivity for Context

Getting stuck in rigid coherence and literality, relying too much on self-imposed rules, being fused with fixed self-labels, and avoiding direct experiences all reduce a person's adaptability, making them less responsive to changing environments. This context insensitivity limits awareness of the factors influencing behavior—both internal and external, and occurring before or after a given action (Villatte et al., 2015).

For example, before trying something new, a person might be influenced by encouragement or discouragement from others, or by their own internal feelings—such as confidence that things will go well or anxiety that they will fail. After trying something new, the person might feel joy and pride, or sadness and regret, depending on the outcome and their interpretation of it. All of these factors will shape their future behavior. The more aware someone is of their context, the better they can adapt and make conscious choices that align with their values. This sensitivity helps them discern when bold actions are appropriate and when restraint might be wiser.

However, individuals with low context sensitivity often fall into an unhelpful cycle, defaulting to familiar behaviors and rigid internalized rules. They rely on what they think they know, without questioning their assumptions or beliefs. As previously discussed, the mind craves consistency, particularly in challenging situations. When faced with stress, people tend to revert to behaviors and beliefs that align with their self-story. However, relying on only one default behavior—such as "not speaking up," "always being kind," or "always being aggressive"—can lead to failure in situations that require a different approach. Flexibility is key.

4.4 Impact on Self-as-Context

When the ability to recognize and name one's own inner processes (self-as-process) is impaired, and there is a strong fusion with one's self-image (self-as-content), adopting the observer perspective on oneself or others (self-as-context) becomes challenging. Clients who struggle with self-as-process often exhibit limitations in the following areas:

- Adopting flexible perspectives on themselves and others
- Practicing self-compassion and compassion for others

- Motivating themselves through larger goals or values

Examining the development of these processes can clarify why these difficulties arise.

4.4.1 Focus Turns to the Caregiver

Children require attention and reliable feedback to unfold their rich inner world and learn to navigate it. They quickly learn whether they receive unconditional love and care, or whether they must earn such things. When attention is rare and conditional, a child is left with little feedback or guidance about their inner experiences. So, the child's focus shifts toward their caregivers:

- "What are their needs?"
- "What do they expect?"
- "How can I meet these expectations to get more attention?"
- "How do I protect myself from harm?"

The child's attention shifts away from their own internal feedback system. They may attempt to please their parents, become rebellious, or withdraw—whatever works to gain more attention and/or security. Once these behaviors are successful, they often become habitual and rigid. However, these patterns will not always be beneficial in every situation, and can even be harmful at times. As a result, the child misses out on developing the broad range of behaviors needed to handle life's diverse challenges.

In such cases, the ability to maintain contact with oneself—recognizing which actions are acceptable for oneself and which ones cross personal boundaries—while simultaneously engaging with others often remains underdeveloped. This challenge frequently persists well into adulthood, where it can impact people's relationships. Orientation then occurs less through internal perception and more through external cues, such as orienting to others' expectations or adhering to rigid childhood rules. These rules may not be helpful in the current situation and can maintain an unfavorable status quo. For instance, following the rule "I should always do what my partner wants, even if it goes against my own wishes, or I'll get into trouble" can be just as harmful in a relationship as rigidly adhering to "I never do what someone else tells me to because I am a free person."

4.4.2 When Social Contact Becomes Threatening

We need perspective-taking to develop a good relationship to ourselves and others, and we need self-as-process skills as the foundation for perspective-taking. When a client hasn't learned to understand their own inner experiences, interpret the social language of emotions, share their feelings, or cultivate compassion for themselves and others, social interactions can feel deeply unsettling, triggering anxiety or even aggression. Imagine being in a foreign country where you barely speak the language and have no map or compass to guide you. It's a scary experience, and this is similar to how the client might feel. They may struggle to comprehend why others behave in certain ways or to predict how they might act. In such a scenario, social contact is not enjoyable or nurturing, and instead becomes a constant challenge, requiring immense effort to navigate.

4.4.3 Passivity and Motivation

Perspective-taking is also key for generating long-term goals and life directions, which can serve as powerful driving forces in life. However, repeated and prolonged negative events in childhood and adulthood can overwhelm an individual's coping capacity. Neurological research suggests that, when faced with such overwhelming events, a person may default to a state of anxiety and passivity (Maier & Seligman, 2016). According to the concept of coherence, the person may stop trying to be active or improve their situation. And this resignation is compounded when they compare themself to others who appear more successful, thus intensifying feelings of inadequacy. The lack of support from significant others in dealing with inner experiences, along with the inability to take a perspective on oneself and others, contributes to the vicious cycle.

Fortunately, when life circumstances improve—such as when a person receives guidance in therapy or from supportive people in their life—they can learn that they are capable of handling painful events, that these events will pass, and that life can improve again. Maier and Seligman (2016) refer to this as the "hope circuit," which can be cultivated and applied to future challenges.

In therapy, you can guide clients in developing these essential skills. For instance, you can help them recognize that they ("I-here") are feeling helpless and sad in the moment ("now"), and explore how those feelings may echo similar experiences from the past ("I-then"). They can observe themselves with some distance, noticing similar feelings of helplessness and sadness in different situations. They ("I-here") can anticipate feeling better in the future ("I-then"), knowing that feelings may change over time. And they can foster confidence in their ability to regain agency, even if it currently doesn't feel like they can.

Through therapeutic processes like acceptance and self-as-context, combined with a focus on what is valuable enough for them to face their pain, your clients can gradually learn to experience themselves as capable and self-efficient in the face of difficult challenges.

4.5 Summarized Impact Using the Example of Lisa

A client named Lisa had a difficult childhood. Her mother and father were drug addicts, and she grew up neglected in terms of nutrition, clothing, housekeeping, and emotional care. At the age of four, she began taking care of her younger brother, collecting deposit bottles to buy food, preparing meals, and dressing herself and her brother. The apartment was filled with garbage and bugs. Lisa's first memory of primary school is the other children saying, "You stink." The pain of this moment was so intense that she could hardly bear it. She needed a mother to turn to—someone with whom she could share her sorrow, someone who would embrace her, name the pain, say, "Wow, this really hurts!" and confirm that it wasn't okay for the other children to say such things. All of this would have helped Lisa handle the situation more flexibly. But no one cared about Lisa's sorrow, and she dared not approach her mother, as her mother would occasionally become violent or dismiss her by telling her not to be such a baby. Her father passed away when she was eight, and her mother had various partners who either ignored or mistreated Lisa. The family moved more than thirty times whenever the mother could no longer afford the rent. Lisa never found a stable circle of friends.

Years later, Lisa came to therapy overworked, depressed, and unable to feel her bodily signals. One of her first statements was that she wasn't willing to experience difficult emotions. She sought therapy not to explore her feelings but to stop overworking herself.

4.5.1 Self-as-Process

When Lisa spoke about her work overload, a difficult feeling arose. I acknowledged that she preferred to not deal with difficult emotions. However, since the feeling was persistent, I suggested we slow down and take a moment to explore it together. Having developed some trust, she agreed. I asked her to describe what she felt in her body and if she could name the emotion. She replied, "I don't know, it just feels bad," which is a typical answer from a client who hasn't learned to perceive, name, structure, and regulate their inner world. Similar statements include "I can't feel anything in my body" and "I only feel this in my head." Excessive rumination can also be part of it, where the person tries to "resolve" the difficult emotion, even though emotions are not problems that the mind can resolve.

In her childhood, Lisa had to check on her parents and her mother's later partners every day: "Are they angry?" "Are they satisfied with me?" "Will they hit me?" There was no space for self-inquiry like "What is my favorite food?" "What do I want to play?" "How do I feel?" or "What do I need?" Lisa never learned that her internal world mattered to anyone, so she didn't care about it either. She never truly learned to use her inner feedback as the helpful navigation system it was meant to be.

Lisa's home was the most dangerous place in her childhood, as her parents mistreated her more than her peers. In therapy, she noticed that her "emotional monsters" always appeared when she was at home after work and wanted to relax. Her home didn't feel like a safe place, and she realized that this contributed to her relentless compulsion to stay active, even at home. She avoided getting present with the fear and pain from her childhood. It took a long period of practicing acceptance with these difficult feelings before she could say, "There is this terrible feeling. It's my old pain. I can allow it, and it will pass. Today, I am safe at home."

4.5.2 Self-as-Content

Lisa's emotional numbness was a necessary survival strategy during her childhood. Expressing her needs to her violent parents would have been dangerous, so her mind learned to ignore those feelings. Once the mind learns such a survival strategy, it tends to keep it as a permanent truth. Unfortunately, as she grew into adulthood, this same strategy led Lisa to burnout and depression, as she didn't pay attention to when she overworked herself or when painful events occurred. When a person's internal compass is inaccessible, their perception of the external world becomes limited. Lisa missed opportunities to relax because she always saw what else needed to be done in her home. Relaxation was not part of her experiences up until that point, and it took two years of therapy before she could sit on her sofa and enjoy a cup of tea for fifteen minutes.

Lisa also had a strong belief that others didn't like her and that she was unlovable. No matter how much she worked or how much she cared for others, she often felt worthless. Her automatic behaviors, aimed at fulfilling her unmet needs, led to more of what she wanted to avoid. Her relationships with friends and partners often ended in disappointment. She was the one who invested a lot, and everyone came to her with their problems, but when she needed someone, others were not there for her—or even left her. She had no idea why this was the case or why others behaved so incomprehensibly and unfairly. It wasn't until therapy that she realized she often chose friends to whom she felt superior, and that she didn't truly open up and show vulnerability. These friends, in turn, were not really interested in an open, equal relationship either.

4.5.3 Self-as-Context

As a child, Lisa became an expert at figuring out what was going on with her parents and with other people. However, since she wasn't in touch with herself during this process, this social skill didn't help her form fulfilling relationships. Her perspective on others was present but narrow, focused on features like "What do they need?" and "Are they kind or aggressive?" Her perspective on herself was lacking, along with self-compassion and a broader view of others. Instead of orienting herself by her actual experiences, Lisa, throughout her adult life, adhered to the rules that had proven helpful to her as a child, such as "Care for others first," "Don't care about your own feelings," and "Work hard, never relax." Since Lisa could remember, she had been overwhelmed by the workload of taking care of herself, her brother, the household, and school. This became her habit and role, which continued into her adult relationships.

Despite her ability to quickly assess how others were feeling and what they needed, Lisa appeared indifferent and lacking in empathy in our contact. Her ability to take on others' perspectives had been tied to the purpose of providing her with security and attention since childhood. She perceived others for the sake of herself, excluding many other internal and external perceptions. There wasn't much compassion for others' needs or awareness of her impact on others, nor any awareness that these qualities were missing. Later, in therapy, she described it as living in a bubble—often lonely, not understanding why she couldn't truly connect with others or why others withdrew from her.

At first glance, Lisa appeared highly motivated in life. She consistently delivered the most reliable and highest performance among her colleagues, even taking on the work of others who were slower. She was clear that she wanted to find a suitable partner and have children who would have a better life than she did. Furthermore, she engaged excessively in exercise.

However, her motivation was strongly driven by avoidance and clinging: avoiding negative feedback from superiors, avoiding conflicts, avoiding her vulnerability and painful feelings related to her upbringing and ongoing struggles, and clinging to good feelings of achievement in sports. This motivation led to overwork, health problems, and uncertainty in partner choice. Lisa consistently avoided her inner experiences, which would have provided her with clues about when she was pushing her physical limits or which partner made her feel secure.

Lisa also tended to trust partners who turned out to be uncaring or even aggressive. These experiences led her to become even more distrustful of people and dismissive in situations where she could have had positive experiences. Her behavior, in turn, was often incomprehensible and unpleasant to others.

These cycles are not easily broken. It takes a lot of practice and many social interactions to disrupt these patterns. Therapy was a safe place for Lisa to try out new interactions and receive honest, helpful feedback. The more she acted courageously, the more she discovered that life in the present was far less threatening than it seemed. Each new action expanded her behavioral repertoire, opening doors to new possibilities, allowing her to make peace with herself and her past. Relationships remained a significant challenge for her, but she learned to cultivate greater awareness and compassion for both herself and others. She became more able to express her emotions, and her relationships grew more open, stable, and mutually fulfilling.

4.6 Summary

The impact of a child experiencing rigid cues, a lack of cues, or invalidating and even hostile cues can reach into adulthood and manifest in all three self-aspects. Possible manifestations in each area include:

Self-as-Process

- Missing emotional labels and regulation capacities: Without the ability to identify and name emotions, a person's feelings can become overwhelming and threatening, making it difficult to process them constructively.
- Emotional avoidance: To escape this discomfort, individuals may avoid engaging with their emotions altogether. This avoidance restricts the exchange between the inner and outer worlds, creating feedback loops that reinforce unfavorable self-stories.
- Lost inner compass: When emotions and needs are not recognized or validated, an individual's ability to make confident decisions diminishes, leaving them uncertain and disconnected from their own values and preferences.

Self-as-Content

- Heightened coherence and literality: Individuals may cling rigidly to coherence and literal interpretations of experiences, reinforcing negative self-stories and beliefs.
- Insensitivity to context: This rigidity often prevents flexible, context-sensitive actions, leading to ineffective or inappropriate responses in different situations.
- Self-labeling and rigid self-rules: Internalized negative self-labels ("I am unlovable," "I am not enough") and inflexible rules ("I must always put others first") dominate, limiting adaptive behaviors.
- Coherence, literal thinking, self-labels, and self-rules persist for several reasons (Villatte et al., 2015):
    - Coherence is one of our strongest reinforcers.
    - Perception is biased, tending to notice what fits the existing picture and ignore information that contradicts it.
    - We become insensitive to the context of our actions and fail to recognize important cues that could guide us in a new direction.
    - We often don't challenge our rules, preventing us from building new experiences.
    - We seek evidence that supports coherence, even when our experiences suggest otherwise, often dismissing contradictions as exceptions.

Self-as-Context

- Focus on caregivers over self-awareness: Early survival strategies that orient toward caregivers' needs and emotions impede the development of self-perspective. This leaves individuals disconnected from their own inner world and unable to take a balanced observer stance.
- Social contact as a threat: Difficulties interpreting and trusting social cues can make interactions feel intimidating or even hostile, increasing anxiety and withdrawal.
- Passivity and lack of motivation: A history of overwhelming or invalidating experiences can result in a default mode of helplessness, which can leave individuals feeling incapable of initiating meaningful change or pursuing long-term goals, even when opportunities for change are present.

Through the observer perspective, I was able to see my twelve-year-old self with more compassionate eyes. Even ten years later, I still find myself adopting this neutral observer's view in various situations, allowing me to gain the necessary distance and respond to circumstances in a much more appropriate way.

—Veronika, thirty-seven years old, medical assistant

CHAPTER 5

Bringing Evolution to Psychotherapy

When we hear the word "evolution," we often think of humanity's broad, collective development. But every person undergoes their own evolution throughout their lifespan. And as therapists, we aim to support this process in ways that are meaningful to our clients, which, in turn, can influence society as a whole (Hayes, Hofmann, & Wilson, 2020).

In this chapter, we extend the ACT framework by incorporating insights from modern evolutionary science, highlighting its advantages. Evolutionary science helps us understand both our origins and our future—insights that are essential in psychotherapy. As therapists, we explore our clients' personal histories, their life circumstances, and the broader contexts shaping their current experiences. At the same time, we help uncover their hopes and goals, identify behaviors they wish to cultivate, and support their ongoing growth.

In the following section, we will explore how the three self-processes are applied in therapeutic practice and discuss the additional benefits of integrating an evolutionary perspective—particularly in identifying clients' inflexibility across the core ACT processes and the different levels of biophysiological and sociocultural functioning.

5.1 A Uniting Evolutionary Model

The extended evolutionary meta model (EEMM) is a framework that aims to provide common ground for practitioners from different therapeutic orientations. Over the past few decades, psychotherapy has seen the rise of diverse approaches, each offering unique insights into clients' lives and pathways to healing. However, the time has come for a unified framework to consolidate and amplify our collective knowledge.

Over the course of my years as a therapist, I've often noticed that clients who have already undergone therapy—regardless of the approach—come with a foundation that we can build upon in our sessions. Research confirms that various psychotherapeutic modalities have long-lasting effects (Hofmann et al., 2012; Gloster et al., 2020). Regardless of our specific training, therapists share a common goal: to help clients change their behavior. This can involve overt behaviors, such as adopting new actions, or fostering internal shifts, like reframing their relationships with thoughts or past experiences. Ultimately, we aim to empower clients to make informed choices in the present and sustain meaningful behaviors. These objectives align with the evolutionary principles of variation, selection, and retention, which offer a shared language we can use across modalities.

Variation, selection, and retention are universal concepts that operate effectively at all levels in therapy. When a client feels stuck, introducing variation—such as standing up and engaging in a physical exercise—often sparks productive progress. For instance, when a client struggles to achieve a certain goal, we might explore different approaches. The client might symbolically define the goal in my therapy room (e.g., using a large plant to represent it) and experiment with different ways of moving toward it. They might walk, jump, dance, crawl, or even move backward—each representing a new variation (originally developed by Rainer Sonntag in a supervision session, 2011). This process reliably generates ideas for new behaviors. And while this exercise may not deliver a complete solution, it often suggests a first step, which the client then chooses (what we call "selection"). We evaluate this step in a subsequent session—assessing its success—and then consider options to sustain this new behavior (referred to as "retention").

These three principles also come into play during the initial consultation. Clients often find it difficult to even imagine acting differently. As therapists, we create space and encourage them to consider that they can learn new behaviors (variation). Together, we discuss their goals (selection) and explore how to achieve and maintain them (retention). I emphasize the willingness to engage in experiential exercises, to practice in daily life, and to establish lasting new structures to clarify that new behaviors do not magically emerge from lengthy conversations.

Psychopathology is almost always linked to rigid behavior patterns. These might include depressive behaviors like withdrawal, self-criticism, and lack of motivation; compulsive behaviors such as repeatedly checking all the electrical appliances in the house before bed; or emotionally unstable behaviors like intense outbursts and abrupt relationship terminations (Ciarrochi et al., 2024). Therefore, promoting variation, which leads to greater psychological and behavioral flexibility, is a crucial first step in therapy.

5.1.1 EEMM Processes and Levels

The EEMM focuses on the core processes that drive successful therapy, regardless of the specific therapeutic approach (Hofmann, Hayes, & Lorscheid, 2021; Ong, Ciarrochi, Hofmann, Karekla, & Hayes, 2024). This model is based on an extensive scientific effort that systematically reviewed and reexamined nearly all factors shown to be effective in psychology studies, organizing them into coherent clusters (Hayes, Ciarrochi, Hofmann, Chin, & Sahdra, 2022). From the condensed analyses, the six core processes of psychological flexibility emerged:

- Acceptance: Represented by "Affect" ("I feel helpless and spend many hours in bed every day.")
- Defusion: Represented by "Cognition" ("Ruminating prevents me from doing what matters to me.")
- Self-as-context: Represented by "Self" ("I am a loser and don't dare to connect to others.")
- Presence: Represented by "Attention" ("I cannot concentrate at work.")
- Values: Represented by "Motivation" ("Why should I bother?")
- Committed action: Represented by "Overt Behavior" or "Action" ("I scream a lot at my children, whom I love.")

In addition to these six core processes, two additional levels have emerged as essential components:

- Relationships and culture ("My husband says I don't support him," "I am bullied at work because of my skin color.")
- Biology and physiology ("I have a chronic disease," "I drink alcohol every day after work.")

These factors make intuitive sense. Every evidence-based therapeutic method works with the core psychological processes—affect, cognition, self, attention, motivation, and action—and in daily practice, we can see how much clients' behaviors are influenced by their social and cultural background, family history, genetic dispositions, sleep quality, eating habits, and more.

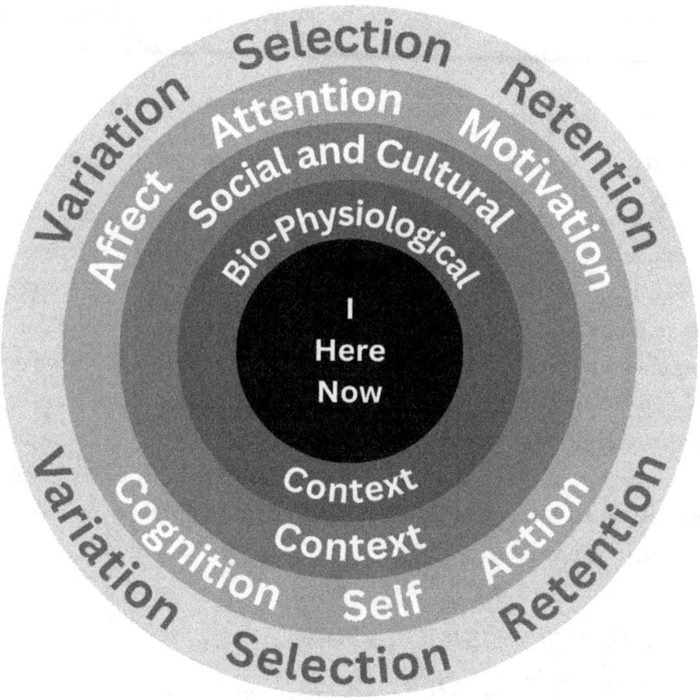

Figure 1: The Extended Evolutionary Meta Model (EEMM)
Adapted by Ebert, B. (Design by Lorscheid, D.)

The EEMM isn't intended to replace existing therapy approaches, but rather to serve as a meta model, offering a common ground for clinicians. In this model, the individual self (I-here-now) evolves its psychological dimensions (affect, cognition, attention, self, values, and action) within the interactive space between biological and physical conditions, and social and cultural environments.

The overarching structure of the model is guided by the evolutionary principles of variation, selection, and retention:

- Variation: Expanding the client's behavioral options.
- Selection: Choosing behaviors aligned with values-based motivations.
- Retention: Establishing and sustaining desirable behaviors over time.

By examining your client's patterns of flexibility or inflexibility across the EEMM dimensions, you can assess their situation and the context of the behaviors they want to change, helping to generate targeted interventions. The six dimensions and two levels of the EEMM form an interrelated network. When a client experiments with new behavior in one dimension, it impacts other areas as well. The goal is to identify key points within this network to disrupt rigid patterns in a way that facilitates growth in the desired direction.

5.1.2 EEMM and Self-Aspects

The dimensions of the EEMM can be examined in relation to the three aspects of the self:

- Self-as-process: The client's capacity to be aware of and describe their ongoing experiences and actions.
- Self-as-content: The client's flexible or rigid relationship to their self-narratives.
- Self-as-context: The client's awareness of their own perspective and other possible perspectives.

Unlocking these self-capacities depends on an individual's personal history and may vary across different EEMM levels and situations. For example, a person may excel at naming and categorizing their inner experiences and understanding others' perspectives in everyday relationships. However, if they have experienced violence, they may struggle to access these skills when confronted with aggression. Another person might be highly aware of their internal experiences but find it challenging to manage strong emotions or adopt a more distant perspective. Conversely, some clients may easily adopt a distant perspective on themselves but struggle to fully experience and process their emotions. Our primary focus is on whether clients can adapt their behavior across various situations in ways that align with their values.

5.1.3 Identifying Fusion Across EEMM Dimensions and Self-Aspects

It is important to note that strong fusion with self-content and low abilities in self-as-process and self-as-context can negatively impact clients in all six dimensions and two levels of the EEMM. The rigid self-concept works like a straitjacket that keeps the client locked in. Practicing self-as-process and self-as-context extensively is key in upgrading the client's self-capacities and loosening their limiting self-beliefs.

In your assessment with a client, you can identify inflexibility in the three self-aspects across the EEMM dimensions by using targeted questions (see table 1). Also, refer to examples for rigid self-content across the EEMM dimensions (see table 2).

Table 1: Identify Flexibility/Inflexibility in the Three Self-Aspects Across EEMM Dimensions

	Self-as-Process	**Self-as-Content**	**Self-as-Context**
Affect	Can clients notice and name a wide range of their emotions, and how much does that ability depend on certain conditions? Are certain emotions related to specific thoughts and/or situations? Are clients aware of those context factors?	What do clients say about their emotions? How much do they identify with their emotions? Are their emotions fluid and variable, or are clients stuck in and overwhelmed by certain emotions, reinforcing rigid self-content?	Can clients take distant and flexible perspectives on their emotions? Can clients accept and integrate challenging emotions as part of their sense of self? Are clients' actions dictated by emotions, or are they consciously chosen in alignment with values?
Cognition	Can clients notice and name a wide range of their thoughts, and how much does that ability depend on certain conditions? Are certain thoughts related to specific emotions and/or situations? Are clients aware of those context factors?	What do clients say about their thoughts? How much do they identify with their thoughts? Are their thoughts creative and variable, or are clients stuck in rumination, reinforcing rigid self-content?	Can clients take distant and flexible perspectives on their thoughts? Can clients accept and integrate challenging thoughts as part of their sense of self? Are clients' actions dictated by thoughts, or are they consciously chosen in alignment with values?

	Self-as-Process	**Self-as-Content**	**Self-as-Context**
Attention	Can clients attend to the moment-to-moment process inside and outside themselves, and how much does that ability depend on certain conditions? Is attentional shifting possible or not? Are clients aware of context factors that facilitate attentional shifting?	What do clients say about what they attend to? Do clients overly attend to, or avoid attending to, certain internal or external experiences? Do these overly attended or avoided experiences reinforce rigid self-content?	Can clients take a distant and flexible perspective on how they attend to their experiences? Can clients accept and integrate overly attended or avoided experiences as part of their sense of self? Can clients flexibly direct their attention toward their valued purposes, both alone and in relationships?
Self	Can clients notice and name a wide range of their internal and external experiences (e.g., bodily sensations, emotions, thoughts, actions), and how much does that ability depend on certain conditions? Is the ability to notice certain experiences related to specific situations? Are clients aware of those context factors?	What do clients say about themselves? How much do they identify with their self-image? Is their self-image flexible, giving space for learning and development, or is it narrowed, rigid, and lacking autonomy?	Can clients take distant and flexible perspectives on themselves and self-related content? Can clients accept and integrate challenging aspects of self-content without becoming fused with them? Are clients able to take others' perspectives and still be grounded in their own perspective? Do clients experience a steady inner core and, from this foundation, foster supportive, valuable relationships?

	Self-as-Process	**Self-as-Content**	**Self-as-Context**
Motivation	Can clients notice their moment-to-moment motivations and their overarching values, and how much does that ability depend on certain conditions? Are clients aware of context factors that strengthen or weaken their contact with motivations and values?	What do clients say about their values and goals? Do they overly identify with, ignore, or flexibly approach their values and goals? Can they consciously choose how to invest their time and energy, or are they driven to reinforce rigid self-content?	Can clients take distant and flexible perspectives on their valued purposes and goals? Can clients accept and integrate challenges related to their motivation and valued direction? Can clients use their valued purposes as a source of guidance and strength?
Overt Behavior	Can clients notice and name a wide range of possible overt behaviors, and how much does that ability depend on certain conditions? Are certain overt behaviors related to specific bodily sensations, emotions, thoughts, and/or situations? Are clients aware of those context factors?	What do clients say about their overt behaviors? How much do they identify with their overt behaviors? Do clients' overt behaviors open up new possibilities for learning and developing, or do they reinforce rigid self-content?	Can clients take distant and flexible perspectives on their overt behaviors? Can clients accept and integrate challenges related to their overt behaviors? Can clients act competently in the direction of their chosen values, both alone and in relationships?

	Self-as-Process	Self-as-Content	Self-as-Context
Biology and Physiology	Can clients notice and name the ongoing flow of physical feedback in their body, and how much does that ability depend on certain conditions? Are clients aware of specific physical, neurological, genetic, and other biological conditions that influence their behavior?	What do clients say about their physical and biological conditions? How much do they identify with those conditions? Do clients relate to their physical and biological conditions flexibly, or in a way that reinforces rigid self-content?	Can clients take distant and flexible perspectives on their physical and biological conditions? Can clients accept and integrate challenges related to their physical and biological conditions? Can clients act competently in the direction of their chosen values, while navigating their physical and biological conditions?
Sociocultural Functioning	Can clients notice and name their ongoing social experiences and cultural influences, and how much does that ability depend on certain conditions? Do clients notice specific social and cultural conditions that influence their behavior?	What do clients say about their social experiences and cultural influences? How much do they identify with those experiences and influences? Do clients relate to their social experiences and cultural influences flexibly, or in a way that reinforces rigid self-content?	Can clients take distant and flexible perspectives on their social experiences and cultural influences? Can clients accept and integrate challenges related to their social experiences and cultural influences? Can clients act competently in the direction of their chosen values, while navigating their social experiences and cultural influences?

Table 2: Examples of Rigid Self-Content Across EEMM Dimensions

	Examples of Rigid Self-Content
Affect	"I am overly emotional." "I'm the kind of person who gets angry easily." "I'm lost in a deep sea of sadness."
Cognition	"I'm such a loser." "I often think that I am a bad mom. With my history, I can't get it right." "Being at the top still isn't good enough."
Attention	"I have ADHD; I can't focus." "I'm always focused on what others need." "I can't stop thinking about gaming again."
Self	*Self-rules and self-labels:* "If I don't perform well, it means I'm a failure." "I am broken." "Why should someone like me even be alive?" *Comparisons and ideals:* "I should be as productive as my business partner." "I'm too big; I should look like my sister—she's always been the slim one." *Predictions about the future:* "With this trauma, I can never be happy." "That's just how I am, and I don't think anyone can help me."
Motivation	"I always procrastinate." "I can't motivate myself." "I don't care." "I'm a rebel and always do the opposite of what others say."
Overt Behavior	"My ex-partner mistreated me, but I still respond to his messages." "I always start something new, but never finish it." "I've tried to quit smoking cigarettes and weed multiple times, but I never succeed." "I hide away in my job." "I've spent most of the day in bed for the last fifteen months."
Biology and Physiology	"I am an alcoholic, just like my dad." "Because of my disability, I can't be a caring daughter to my parents." "I can't escape post-COVID and the fatigue it brings."

	Examples of Rigid Self-Content
Sociocultural Functioning	"I am discriminated against because I am autistic." "I scream at my wife." "In my culture, men don't admit or show emotions." "I feel like an alien." "I cannot open up here in therapy."

In the next part of the chapter, we will explore how these dynamics might present in a client to better understand their practical implications.

5.2 Processes in Action: Hamdi

Hamdi is a young man in his early twenties who has completed training as a gardener. He holds a secure, well-paid job in the public sector. Born in Germany with roots in an Arabic Muslim culture, Hamdi sought therapy to address daily panic attacks, persistent rumination, and significant sleep disturbances, all of which left him feeling desperate.

The panic attacks began a few months earlier, following the sudden death of a close friend from an undetected medical condition. Additionally, Hamdi feels that his supervisor assigns him undesirable tasks and treats him in a racist manner. Despite these challenges, he enjoys his profession and gets along well with his colleagues.

To avoid nighttime panic attacks, Hamdi spends hours watching videos in the evening. He then consumes ten to fifteen cups of coffee daily to stay awake at work. Over the past few years, he has used drugs and alcohol once or twice a month, primarily on weekends. At times—when he is using substances—he gets in physical altercations, especially when he perceives others as disrespectful. Hamdi's substance use escalated after his panic attacks began, as it temporarily relieved his anxiety. However, he describes the following day as "hell," marked by headaches, dullness, and listlessness. He believes that drug use is worsening his panic attacks in the long term.

Hamdi views himself as a "bad person" due to his involvement in brawls and has considered quitting drugs, at least temporarily. However, despite his efforts to stop, he often relapses when meeting friends, convincing himself that he "can control it." He worries about disappointing his parents with his behavior.

The youngest of five brothers, he recalls being ignored or teased by his older siblings for his love of plants and animals. Determined to become stronger and no longer be subjected to ridicule, he began training in martial arts, becoming a muscular young man who discovered that others respected him most when he displayed physical strength.

Although raised in a liberal Muslim family, Hamdi is not a practicing Muslim. Emotional expression was not emphasized in his upbringing, and his family rarely addressed feelings or provided examples of how to handle difficult emotions openly or flexibly. As a result, Hamdi struggles to identify a broad range of emotions and lacks strategies for managing them effectively.

Now in therapy, Hamdi seeks practical advice and clear solutions to alleviate his fear, hoping for straightforward guidance to make his panic attacks disappear. In the therapeutic relationship, he appears friendly and approachable.

5.2.1 Inflexible Behavior

Affect:

- Hamdi's ability to perceive and label his emotions is limited. He predominantly notices a narrow range of intense emotions: panic and fear related to his panic attacks, fear of illness and death, relief after using drugs, and anger when confronted with disrespectful behavior.
- He has little or no access to more vulnerable emotions, such as helplessness in the face of his fears or sadness over the loss of his friend. Similarly, he struggles to acknowledge feelings of shame, humiliation, or disappointment regarding his mistreatment at work. On rare occasions, he mentions his care for plants and animals, or the joy he derives from his work as a gardener.
- Hamdi tends to either avoid uncomfortable emotions or feel overwhelmed by them, particularly fear. He also forms faulty rules about his emotions, believing they dictate his behavior. For example; he assumes, "If the fear is so great, I need to drink alcohol; otherwise, I can't go out." In reality, while he is capable of going out despite feeling anxious, the experience is so distressing that he chooses not to.

Cognition:

- Hamdi tries to find solutions by rumination.
- He has recurring thoughts about why his friend had to die so early and whether the same fate could befall him.
- He is dwelling on the supervisor's behavior, recognizing it as racial discrimination, and feeling that the situation is unfair.

Attention:

- Hamdi's attention is narrowly focused on his fear and on avoiding further panic attacks and difficult emotions.
- He prioritizes short-term relief, such as thinking, "When I drink alcohol, my anxiety gets better," or, "If I watch videos long enough, I fall asleep deeply and avoid panic attacks."
- He neglects to attend to the medium- and long-term consequences, like how his lack of sleep leaves him tired, unfocused, and irritable, escalating conflicts with his supervisor and increasing his stress.
- He also ignores how distress and excessive coffee consumption raise the likelihood of future panic attacks.

Self:

- Hamdi struggles to adopt a distanced perspective on himself, especially when he feels fearful, panicked, or angry. He strongly identifies with self-statements like "I am scared of having a severe illness and dying," "I sometimes get very angry and want to protect weaker people," "I am a bad person because of my brawls," and "I make my parents unhappy."

- As a child, Hamdi saw himself as weak and helpless, often retreating into his love of plants and animals to cope with the teasing and attacks from his four older brothers. As an adult, he views emotions like anxiety, helplessness, and sadness as weaknesses that he believes he should not experience.
- His physical strength has become a significant part of his identity, providing him with pride, security, and a sense of superiority. An implicit self-rule may exist, such as: "When I am strong, I can control my life." However, the sudden death of his friend has disrupted this belief, forcing Hamdi to confront his vulnerability and mortality—concepts he had scarcely considered before.
- Hamdi lacks self-compassion and has not acknowledged the depth of his sadness for losing his friend. He engages in minimal self-reflection, struggling to process his emotions constructively.

Motivation:

- Respecting others—including animals and plants—has always been important to Hamdi. He strives to live peacefully and build relationships based on equality.
- Having a good relationship with his close family is a key value for Hamdi. However, it is intertwined with the internalized rule that he should not disappoint his parents.
- In his current crisis, Hamdi perceives himself as weak willed and lacking motivation, especially after drug abuse.
- When he is emotional, he either disconnects from his values or acts on them in ways that contradict other values (e.g., engaging in physical fights, undermining his value of treating others respectfully).

Overt Behavior/Action:

- Hamdi's current actions are largely dictated by his emotions, emotional avoidance, or rumination (e.g., watching videos, drinking alcohol, using drugs, and engaging in fights). His aggressive behavior, often triggered by alcohol or drug use, contradicts his values and results in difficult emotions like shame.
- His strategies do not address the root of his problems; instead, they worsen his problems and block helpful new perspectives on his fear. Additionally, Hamdi creates faulty connections, such as "Because I'm so afraid, I have to drink alcohol—otherwise I can't bear it."
- In therapy sessions, Hamdi spends much time talking at length, sharing his thoughts, without noticing whether the therapist is following his train of thought. This indicates that he is more connected to his own internal dialogue than to the shared interaction, which might also apply to his other relationships.

Biology/Physiology:

- Hamdi has significant sleep disturbances and relies on excessive amounts of coffee to stay awake.
- He has neglected his martial arts training—which previously provided relaxation—in the last months, contributing to the vicious circle of fear, excessive video consumption, substance abuse, and sleeplessness.
- He is exhausted at work and unable to concentrate, which exacerbates his trouble with his supervisor.

Sociocultural Functioning:

- Hamdi recognizes that the conflict with his supervisor is an example of being discriminated against for racist reasons. Having experienced racist discrimination before, he strongly rejects and finds such behavior unacceptable. In the current situation, however, he sees no way to address or control the discriminatory behavior, nor does he consider other factors that might also contribute to his supervisor's dissatisfaction—factors more within his control, such as his sleepiness and lack of concentration at work.
- Hamdi's self-image reflects the interplay of the different cultures in which he was raised. As a child, he felt inadequate when compared to the masculine ideal in Arab culture, represented by his older brothers. Despite this, he finds comfort and a sense of belonging within his family and their liberal values. In school, Hamdi made friends easily, and he maintains a circle of reliable friends.

5.2.2 Variation: Progress in Therapy

After the first session, we identified two major areas where we could bring variation to Hamdi's behavior. The technical terms are for you; I don't use them with clients:

1. Strengthening self-as-process: Practicing the recognition and naming of a broader range of feelings—including the emotions he had been avoiding—is foundational for developing other skills. Hamdi had not adequately learned this before, and doing so would connect him more deeply with himself and his lived experience in the present moment. Practicing acceptance alongside this recognition would also be helpful when consciously perceiving difficult emotions.
2. Strengthening self-as-context: Developing a more distant perspective on himself and his emotions—while staying connected to them—would offer Hamdi relief and reduce his reliance on avoidance behaviors. This broader perspective would also help him access self-compassion, align more closely with his values, and make behavioral changes that reflect those values.

RECOGNIZING AND NAMING EMOTIONS

In session, Hamdi practiced perceiving his body instead of getting stuck in loops of thinking and talking. This led him to experience and name his difficult emotions more directly (practicing flexible attention or self-as-process). With guidance, he quickly recognized and verbalized his emotions as they shifted from moment to moment: "I feel scared." "Now I feel sad." "And now helpless." "And now furious that nobody helps me."

He practiced giving these emotions space through his breath (practicing acceptance), which turned out to be less overwhelming than he had anticipated. Over time, the emotions became less burdensome, and Hamdi felt motivated to apply the exercise at home. He realized how much energy he had been spending on avoiding discomfort. Interestingly, as he allowed himself to feel his anxieties and fear of death, he found that the frequency of his panic attacks began to decrease.

BUILDING AWARENESS AND SELF-COMPASSION

As he began paying more attention to his own inner feedback, Hamdi noticed that he expected to be judged by me for his behavior (practicing self-awareness and perspective-taking), which made him feel uncomfortable. This discomfort was significant because he recognized how much social relationships—and our therapeutic relationship—mattered to him (getting in touch with motivation and values). It was a vulnerable feeling he had previously avoided.

My invitation—"Would you look closely at me and see if you perceive judgment in my view?"—was initially unfamiliar to him. However, he accepted the challenge and found no judgment (practicing self-awareness and perspective-taking). This was an important "other-as-context moment," as Hamdi realized there was someone genuinely kind and interested in him, regardless of what he revealed.

He saw that therapy was not about pleasing me, but about finding peace with himself and his actions (practicing self-as-context). He said that he felt accepted in the therapeutic relationship as he was. Not feeling pushed in a specific direction or having to prove himself gave him the space to discover a clearer, more valued direction for his life.

REDISCOVERING VALUES

Hamdi became more aware of how valuable his daily work was to him, despite the conflict with his supervisor. Through prompts like "What would decent behavior from your supervisor look like to you?" and "What is particularly important to you in this challenging relationship?" Hamdi began to view his problem within a larger context. He saw that mutual respect was important to him, and he found it difficult to accept that others, such as his supervisor, might not share his values (practicing values and perspective-taking).

5.2.3 Selection: Choosing New Actions

Hamdi began observing his fear and shame with greater detachment, recognizing how he had been avoiding these emotions. This awareness helped him rediscover his deep value of inner freedom, reinforcing his commitment to practicing acceptance. He started seeking healthier ways to reduce his arousal in the evenings, such as spending time chatting with his family, going to bed earlier, or listening to podcasts instead of staying awake watching videos.

ADDRESSING AGGRESSIVE BEHAVIOR

In one session, Hamdi recounted an incident where he had slapped a man in a bar for behaving disrespectfully toward a woman. He described the act as something that "just happened," as though it had been carried out by someone other than himself. It took time for him to bridge the disconnect with his self-image and take ownership, acknowledging, "Indeed, it was me doing this, and I don't like it." Hamdi identified the factors contributing to his aggressive behavior: witnessing mistreatment, being with friends who admired his strength, and the prior consumption of alcohol and drugs. This realization motivated him to commit to abstaining from drug use for three months. He decided he could address disrespectful behavior toward a weaker person in different ways, without resorting to violence.

He also recognized how excessive coffee consumption overstimulated his nervous system, making him more prone to panic attacks. Determined to regain control, he decided to give up coffee as well. Hamdi succeeded in both efforts, which gave him a new sense of self-efficacy and control over his actions.

DEVELOPING COMPASSION AND PERSPECTIVE

Hamdi gradually cultivated a more compassionate view of himself by reflecting on the discrimination, cultural tensions, and familial conflicts he had endured, as well as the grief and fear caused by the death of his close friend. He came to accept that there were no simple solutions to the challenges he faced. Instead, he recognized the value of taking deliberate, committed steps to navigate each situation.

EMPOWERMENT IN THE WORKPLACE

Hamdi decided to address his workplace issues by initiating a conversation with his supervisor. He planned to ask why he was always assigned tasks that nobody else wanted to do. Although he was nervous, it was important for him to see that he was not helpless in this relationship, even with the inherent power imbalance. Before he could have the conversation, though, his disliked supervisor surprised him by recommending him for a three-year professional qualification program. This program would lead to a higher income, greater responsibilities, and more creative work—something Hamdi had desired since starting his job.

5.2.4 Retention: Building New Structures

Hamdi integrated brief exercises of recognizing and naming his inner and outer experiences into his daily routine, even doing so while gardening at work. This practice became a key coping strategy for him. The significant reduction in panic attacks that accompanied his decreased alcohol, drug, and coffee consumption, strongly reinforced his commitment to maintain these new behaviors. Better sleep and increased productivity at work further motivated him to sustain these changes.

Hamdi also resumed his martial arts training and spent more time with sports friends who abstained from alcohol and drugs, creating a peer group that supported his healthier habits. The opportunity to pursue the three-year professional qualification program was a fortunate development that not only motivated Hamdi but also improved his perception of his supervisor.

After six therapy sessions, Hamdi felt confident enough to conclude therapy. And while I do not know how he has fared since then, the progress he achieved during therapy suggests he has built a strong foundation for future growth.

5.2.5 Network Analysis: Understanding Influencing Factors

The contextual factors discussed in this chapter are deeply interconnected, mutually influencing one another and shaping the client's behavior across multiple dimensions. As a therapist, you must determine which factors are most relevant for each individual client. Not all factors are equally important in every case. The example of Hamdi illustrates the interplay of multiple factors and levels within the extended evolutionary meta model. The following network analysis (see figure 2) condenses all the information shared by the client during clinical conversations and through questionnaires. The arrows in the diagram represent hypotheses about the mutual influences among these factors.

A network approach better captures human complexity compared to linear cause-and-effect models. Social, physical, emotional, and cognitive abilities are intricately interwoven, and increasing flexibility in one area often creates positive changes in other areas as well.

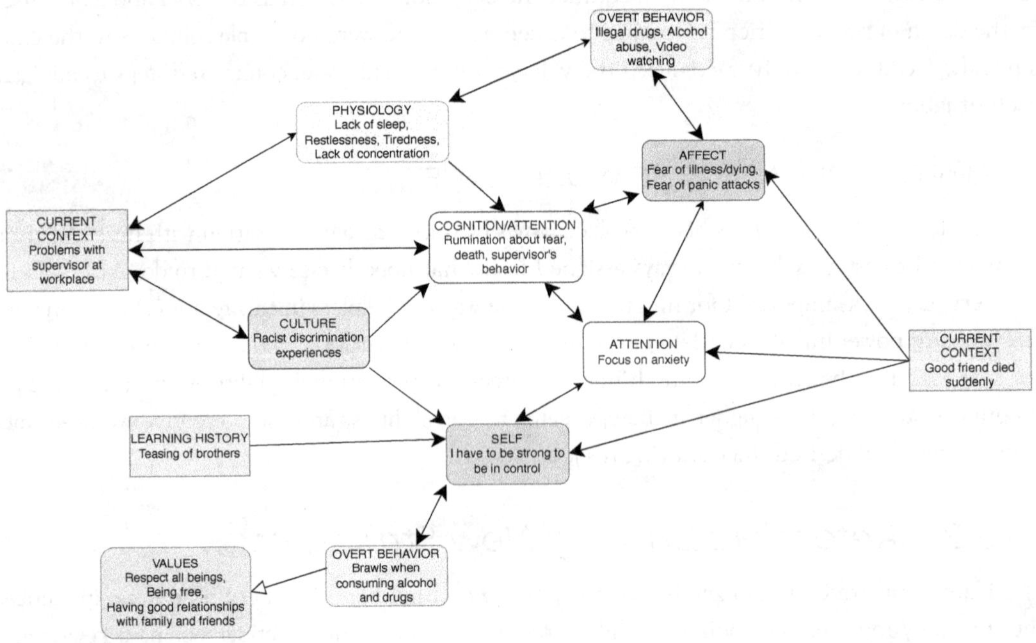

Figure 2: Network analyses based on information shared by client Hamdi

Network analysis often provides clients with an entirely new perspective on what brought them to therapy. Many report that this transparency fosters trust and helps them feel seen. It also gives them the opportunity to challenge my viewpoint, encouraging a collaborative process. Together, we can refine the network and explore how to disrupt unhelpful behavioral patterns in constructive and effective ways.

Delving into the details of network analysis here would exceed the scope of this text, but excellent resources are available on the topic (Hofmann et al., 2021; Ong et al., 2024).

5.3 Sources of Information for Therapeutic Analysis

Being a therapist often feels like working as a detective—carefully piecing together clues to understand the client's complex context. We draw from multiple sources of information:

- Direct experience: The client's behavior in the therapy room and their responses to our questions.
- Therapist feedback: Paying attention to our internal reactions as therapists and evaluating the effectiveness of various interventions.
- Client reports: Listening to clients share insights from their daily lives, relationships, and significant events.
- Emerging behaviors: Noticing new patterns and behaviors that develop as a result of the therapeutic process.
- Collaborative input: Incorporating feedback from colleagues and utilizing assessment measures to gain a broader perspective.

Whatever assessment tools you use, it is essential to remain open and accepting, prioritizing what matters most to the client. Coming to therapy is an act of courage. Opening up to a stranger takes vulnerability and trust. Therapy is a collaborative process where therapist and client explore—with curiosity—what purpose unhelpful behaviors serve in the short and long term, which behaviors could lead to a more fulfilling life, and how to cultivate these more promising alternatives.

5.3.1 Information in Session

In my initial sessions with clients, I prioritize understanding their areas of flexibility and rigidity. My overarching question is: "In which areas and under which circumstances does the client demonstrate more or less psychological flexibility?" Tables 1 and 2 (referenced earlier) hopefully gave you an understanding what questions you can use to address self-related issues.

As therapy progresses, certain patterns tend to emerge when clients are strongly fused with self-as-content:

- When joint efforts with a client fail to bring progress—when acceptance turns into avoidance, when no distance from thoughts is created, and values remain abstract—it often indicates strong inflexibility in their self-image. Such rigidity makes it difficult for the client to consider alternative perspectives, explore new approaches, or develop new skills.

- Sometimes, the client clings so tightly to their self-story that even I, as a therapist, begin to feel convinced that progress is impossible. I may lose curiosity, feeling as though I "already know" them. Every change seems to feel threatening to them, they hardly find new actions they are willing to undertake, and they may repeatedly return to session having done little to implement any changes.
- Clients with a rigid self-story might say things like "Yeah, I know this already" or "I tried what you're proposing earlier, and it didn't work"—a form of control strategy and rejection of interventions that can evoke frustration for us as therapists.
- Another indicator of a rigid self-image is difficulty establishing a therapeutic connection. I may feel distant, uncomfortable, or uncertain about whether I'm taking the right approach, and there may be little sense of a shared process or agreement on the therapeutic direction.

When these patterns emerge, reassess the situation. You might offer simpler tools, such as self-as-process exercises, and break goals down into smaller steps. You can also invite the client to reflect on how you can better support them. In some cases, inpatient treatment may become necessary, or you may need to refer them to another therapist or consider ending therapy when appropriate.

5.3.2 Information from Outside the Therapy Room

As therapists, we spend only a small fraction of time each week with our clients, relying heavily on their accounts of daily life. Every detail they share about their experiences related to long-term self-content is valuable. For example, clients might report:

- New internal experiences: "I've felt more strongly than ever how much I love my children."
- New external observations: "My colleague has been greeting me so kindly; maybe she's been doing it all along, and I just didn't notice."
- Seeing themselves in a broader context: "When I was talking to my daughter, I realized how much I want to be a good role model for her."
- Reconnecting with emotions from the past: "Suddenly, I could feel again what it was like to listen to that incredible punk band, standing in the middle of the crowd, feeling alive from head to toe."
- Feedback from important others: "My daughter said that I have become much calmer and more open in the last months."

Reports from hospital stays or diagnoses from previous practitioners also provide important insights—especially when they suggest an inflexible self-image. For example, a personality disorder diagnosis may point to a self-picture that is rigidly uncertain or overly grandiose, or clients might be diagnosed with a severe, long-standing depression that is often linked to low self-esteem and feelings of helplessness (McHugh et al., 2019). Repeated inpatient stays can lead clients to internalize a self-view as being "seriously ill" or "difficult to treat," which may be an obstacle to effective therapy if the diagnosis becomes a central part of their self-concept.

The risks associated with these labels don't apply only to clients—they also affect us as therapists. We may unconsciously fuse with our clients' diagnoses, perceiving information that aligns with their diagnosis more strongly than information that contradicts it. This "coherence trap" creates a feedback loop, reinforcing the client's existing self-concept and making it harder for them to develop or reveal qualities that contradict it. It's crucial to remain vigilant and avoid viewing diagnoses as absolute truths. Instead, we should view them as simply one perspective—a description of a person who is far more complex than our clinical lens may initially capture.

5.3.3 Assessment Measures for the Self

Your choice of assessment tools for the self will depend on the model you use in therapy. As an ACT clinician, I utilize the Psyflex questionnaire (Gloster et al., 2021). This brief tool measures the six core psychological flexibility processes, with one question for each process. It is quick, easy to administer, and effective for tracking progress. The item for self-as-context is: "Even if thoughts and experiences are confusing me, I can notice something like a steady core inside of me."

There is also the Process-Based Assessment Tool (PBAT), an item pool designed to measure progress in the change processes and dimensions of the EEMM. Available in various languages, the PBAT indirectly assesses an "autonomous, worthy, and competent" sense of self. Recently, the authors added a brief measure for self-compassion and compassion for others, as well as for therapeutic alliance (Ciarocchi et al., 2022; Ciarrochi, Hayes, Hofmann, & Sahdra 2021).

The Functional Self-Discrimination Measure (FSDM) by Styles and Atkins (2018) is a coding system for recognizing client utterances that indicate self-as-perspective skills and values-driven statements. These metrics, especially when combined, predict improved well-being and better emotional regulation.

For further resources, see McHugh and Stapleton's (2021) article, which details additional scales for assessing self-as-context.

5.4 Conclusion

By identifying both flexible and inflexible behaviors, as well as influencing factors, we take an important first step in raising clients' awareness and formulating goals based on values. The next step is behavior change. A common misconception is that insight alone should be enough to change deeply ingrained behaviors. In reality, insight rarely results in significant change without deliberate practice. Each of us has areas in our lives where we know what we'd like to change but struggle to do so, particularly when undesirable behaviors are tied to long-standing habits and our sense of self.

Behavior change requires effort, sustained practice, and a clear understanding of what strategies are most effective. Clients also need compelling reasons to make these efforts—something that makes the hard work feel worthwhile for them. The next chapter will present exercises and techniques I've found helpful over the past twenty years for guiding clients toward building a more flexible and fulfilling sense of self.

5.5 Summary

We approached the three self-aspects through the evolutionary perspective of the extended evolutionary meta model (EEMM), focusing on identifying rigid behaviors, fostering a greater variation of behaviors, selecting effective behaviors, and ensuring their sustainability (retention).

The EEMM encompasses six dimensions (affect, cognition, attention, self, motivation, overt behavior/action) and two interconnected levels (sociocultural and biophysiological). It is a comprehensive model for assessment and change. The dimensions and levels represent the context in which the client lives, providing the framework through which we must consider their behavior.

Examples of questions to identify rigidity in the EEMM dimensions are provided for all three self-processes—self-as-process, self-as-content, and self-as-context.

We also identified the most important sources of information for us as therapists, including observations inside the therapy room, asking targeted questions, listening to clients' reports from outside the therapy room, and utilizing assessment measures.

When we conduct a network analysis, the EEMM approach allows us to demonstrate and acknowledge the complexity of behavior with the client, and to recognize how unfavorable loops hinder behavioral change. The visualization also enhances confidence, as it highlights the different points for effective interventions in the client's unique circumstances.

> Before, I had always tried to keep everything in my life under control. Accepting my thoughts and emotions was extremely helpful. I learned to see them from an observer's perspective and, over time, handle difficult thoughts and feelings more effectively when they arose. For me, this meant that I didn't have to think or feel perfectly before taking action.
>
> —Stefan, fifty-two years old, department head at a technology company

CHAPTER 6

Training a Flexible Sense of Self

How do you put the knowledge in this book into practice? How can your clients connect more deeply with themselves, gaining the freedom to make meaningful decisions and translate them into action? How can they learn to like themselves more—or at least find peace with themselves—while harnessing their strengths for a fulfilling life? And how can they cultivate more successful relationships? This chapter offers practical ideas and guidance for exploring these questions in therapy.

I've compiled my favorite exercises into a "toolbox" for you, which you can expand over time. Alongside these tools, I've provided actionable instructions to help you use each one effectively. Together, we'll explore a range of training techniques—such as exercises, metaphors, and conversational prompts—aligned with the three aspects of the self: self-as-process, self-as-content, and self-as-context.

Although this book is about self-as-context, it is often most effective to begin with foundational skills. After all, you can't build a house without a solid foundation. For this reason, we begin with self-as-process, which emphasizes presence skills. This often involves cultivating acceptance and defusion, especially when transitioning to challenging self-as-content. When we train these skills and perspectives, self-as-context naturally emerges as the overarching perspective, integrating values, committed actions, and relationships.

The different self-aspects are not rigidly separate; they interplay and overlap in each of the training opportunities described in the following sections. Nevertheless, the exercises will focus on one particular aspect at a time.

6.1 Guidelines for Exercises

There are several helpful principles for using exercises in therapy. They reduce barriers to client participation and increase the likelihood of generating valuable experiences and insights.

NATURAL INTEGRATION

Exercises should flow naturally within the context of the conversation. For example:

- "It seems difficult for you to find a helpful perspective—would you like to try an exercise for that?"
- "You mentioned this issue last time, and I thought we could do an exercise related to it."

SEEK PERMISSION, GIVE A CHOICE

Always ask for the client's consent before starting an exercise:

- "Are you comfortable trying something new with this?"
- "What would help you more in this situation, exploring the difficult emotion you described or finding some distance from it? Or both?"

CLARIFY INTENTIONS

Be clear about the purpose of the exercise, whether it's helping the client perceive an emotion more vividly, uncover new perspectives, or deepen their awareness what is valuable to them. Furthermore, stay open to the client's unexpected reactions or insights. There is no "right" or "wrong" way for an exercise to unfold, as long as you stay present with your intention—which can change during the exercise. For example, if a difficult feeling surfaces during a commitment exercise, you may pause to address it with acceptance and return to commitment later.

REINFORCE INSIGHTS

Acknowledge and validate moments when the client connects with the exercise's purpose or has other valuable experiences:

- "It's a big step for you to notice this difficult emotion, even for a moment. Thank you for allowing it and for sharing it with me."
- "You just adopted a new perspective, and it feels freeing—like more space to breathe, even here on my side!"

FACILITATE GENUINE EXPERIENCE

Superficial engagement with an exercise won't lead to meaningful change. The client's conscious experience—including both verbal and nonverbal elements, such as bodily sensations and mental imagery—is essential. To facilitate this process, you can ask guiding questions:

- Can they visualize a difficult experience?
- Can they feel an emotion in their body?
- What is their experience like for them in this moment?

Move at the client's pace—slower, if necessary—to ensure they can fully engage with the process. Take it step by step, allowing the space they need to absorb and reflect on each experience. Every exercise is a curious exploration. Avoid assuming you know what should happen. Instead, let the exercise unfold naturally between you and your client in this unique moment, inviting the best possible outcome aligned with the client's goals.

6.2 Awareness for Self-as-Process

The foundation of our self-experience lies in the ongoing, ever-evolving process of conscious awareness—our awareness of our body, actions, sensory perceptions, feelings, and thoughts. This dynamic awareness forms the basis for practicing more complex self-capacities, such as adopting broader and more diverse perspectives on ourselves and others.

Self-as-process refers to the ability to stay present, enabling us to arrive repeatedly in the moment and connect with ourselves: "What do I experience now?" Any mindfulness exercises in your repertoire can be helpful here, when you encourage clients to perceive and name the present moment and notice the constant movement of thoughts, sensations, and feelings.

Pure self-as-process exercises are relatively rare. More often, you'll transition into perspective-taking—a natural and valuable extension for most clients. The exercises below illustrate this dynamic in practice.

6.2.1 Exercise: Noticing from Outside to Inside

For clients who struggle to perceive certain aspects of themselves or are overly fixated on specific aspects—such as body, feelings, or thoughts—it's important to help them widen their range of perception. This involves practicing underrepresented aspects while connecting them to areas the client already perceives well. Over time, this approach helps clients access a broader spectrum of self-awareness.

You can begin with simple exercises, as I did with a young client who, after a life-threatening accident, realized he had difficulty sensing his feelings and lacked empathy toward others. His goal was to reconnect with his internal emotional feedback. Since he was an athlete and comfortable with physical awareness, we started with body-based exercises.

Exercise

External Awareness

"Can you feel the armrest of the chair under your hands?"

"Can you sense your feet on the ground and how your legs feel in this position?"

Transition to Internal Awareness

"Can you feel how your breath flows through your nose and how your chest rises and falls as you breathe?"

Encouraging Autonomy in Awareness

Therapist: "And what do you notice now?"

Client: "I'm wondering if the stabbing pain in my chest that I briefly felt might be related to my sitting posture."

Therapist: "Ah, now you're noticing a stabbing pain in your chest and thinking about whether it could be related to your posture. Thank you. And what do you notice now?"

Deepening Internal Awareness

Client: "Now I notice the stabbing pain more, and I have a memory of when my girlfriend visited me in the hospital after my accident."

Therapist: "Thank you. Now, the stabbing pain seems connected to your memory of your girlfriend visiting you in the hospital after your accident. What do you notice now?"

Client: "I remember how she cried. She held my hand. She was shocked that I nearly died. It made me realize, wow, this severe accident really happened! It was me in the car, overturning. I had forgotten about that intense moment."

Continue this process for as long as it's meaningful for the client—usually just a few minutes. Tune into the client's experience, trying to feel what they might be feeling. Reinforce new insights by mirroring and acknowledging attentively what the client shares. This approach not only strengthens the client's internal awareness but also opens pathways to connecting emotional, cognitive, and physical experiences in a more integrated way.

Key Points of the Exercise

- Cultivate awareness of the diversity of personal experiences.
- Practice tracing and naming the inner process across all levels—thoughts, memories, feelings, bodily sensations—as well as visible actions and sensory input.
- Validate every perception as meaningful simply because the client perceives and names it. The goal is to train perception across different levels without the need for change or judgment. Emphasize, "It's good that you can perceive that."
- Consider the client's context; for example, avoid starting with body awareness in cases of body image concerns, or focusing on emotional awareness with clients experiencing high anxiety.
- Encourage the client to practice their awareness in various everyday situations. Assigning this practice as homework between sessions can further reinforce their learning and progress.

6.2.2 Exercise: Noticing and Naming

This exercise, by Strosahl and Robinson (2022), is an excellent tool for cultivating presence and flexible attention. It is particularly effective in moments when the client is experiencing heightened emotions or tension.

Exercise

Begin by modeling the exercise yourself. Walk through the therapy room (you could sit too, but walking gives you more perceptions) while shifting your attention among various perceptions, including external sensory perceptions (such as hearing, seeing, or smelling) and internal perceptions (like bodily sensations, emotions, or thoughts). Each perception is given equal attention and treated neutrally:

- "I see the colorful curtain."
- "I hear the cars on the street."
- "I feel my feet on the floor as I walk."
- "I am having the thought that this exercise will hopefully be helpful to you (the client)."
- "I notice my breath."
- "I see the bookshelf."
- "I think that I should read a book for an upcoming presentation."
- "I feel anxious thinking about the presentation."
- "I hear voices outside."
- "I smell the scent of the flowers on the table."

After modeling the exercise, guide your client through it, ensuring they keep shifting their attention fluidly rather than getting stuck on specific thoughts or feelings. If they begin storytelling and evaluating instead of transitioning between perceptions, gently redirect their focus back to the exercise.

Key Points of the Exercise

- Present moment focus: The exercise directs attention to the present moment, fostering openness and flexible shifting among all arising perceptions—rather than staying fixated on specific thoughts or feelings, as clients often do.
- Nurture agency: The exercise enables the client to consciously direct their attention rather than being overwhelmed by a single thought or emotion.
- Promote calmness: By leading the client to focus on the present moment, the exercise naturally decreases high arousal levels, promoting a calmer state of mind.

6.2.3 Exercise: Noticing, Naming, and Accepting

Exercises that involve perception and naming are fundamental steps toward acceptance. We cannot perceive something without acknowledging its presence. Naming it adds another layer of acceptance, as well as often introducing defusion. When a client notices an experience that they struggle to allow, it opens the door to accepting their nonacceptance, which itself can be a step toward greater acceptance.

The following exercise is one of my central tools for helping clients perceive difficult feelings, consciously accept them, and thereby increase their psychological flexibility. It can begin with a challenging experience the client is currently facing, such as emotional or physical discomfort, or with a remembered feeling.

Clients often localize emotions in their torso—particularly around the heart or abdomen—or in the throat, though some clients may feel emotions in their head or throughout their body. This exercise starts wherever the client perceives a difficult sensation, and every perception is equally valid.

Exercise

Breathing Toward the Experience

- "Would it be okay if we give a bit more attention to this challenging inner experience [pain, fear, uncertainty, etc.] that has surfaced right now?"
- If appropriate, I might also say something like, "I am here, and I will try to feel this difficult feeling with you in my body."
- "Where can you locate the center of this experience in your body? Please breathe in and allow your breath to flow toward this experience, creating some space there as you inhale."

Acknowledging the Experience

- "If it feels right to you, you can exhale with an inner 'Yes,' saying internally, 'Yes, for this breath, I am ready to allow this challenging experience in my body.'"
- "Then, breathe in again and allow your breath to flow toward the challenging experience, giving it a bit more space—and exhale with 'Yes, for this breath, I am ready to allow this challenging experience in my body.'"

Focusing on the Present

- "Right now, nothing else is more important than this challenging experience and your breathing. With each inhale, give it more space, and acknowledge it with a 'Yes' on each exhale."
- "There is nothing to achieve, nothing else to do, except to breathe and notice what happens."

Observing Changes

- "What do you notice as you do this? Is the challenging experience changing? Is it getting bigger? Smaller? Staying the same? Is another experience emerging alongside it?"
- "Everything is okay. There's nothing specific that needs to happen. The intention is simply to perceive and allow."

Concluding the Exercise

- "Take a few more breaths and conclude the exercise for yourself. Is there anything you'd like to share?"

Key Points of the Exercise

- Practicing agency: The client learns a new form of ownership—consciously and competently engaging with a difficult experience. This strengthens the acceptance aspect of self-as-process.
- Reducing domination: By allowing the difficult experience, the client often finds that it becomes less dominating and less controlling of their actions.
- Fostering openness: The exercise fosters openness to inner processes and reinforces the idea that challenging emotions or sensations can be tolerated, observed, and given space without needing to be resolved or fought.

6.2.4 Exercise: Expanding Acceptance to Flexible Perspective-Taking

The previous acceptance exercise can be expanded with flexible perspective-taking. It is another exercise I practice with nearly every client at some point. The shifting between self-as-process and self-as-context is a flexibility that clients usually find very helpful and like practicing.

Exercise

Invitation to Expand

- "Would you be willing to try another step?"

Introducing the Observer Perspective

- "You can now perceive your difficult experience in your body. Can you also notice yourself, sitting here, doing this exercise with me?"
- "We could say that you are connecting to your observer perspective. Can you observe that you are allowing your difficult inner experience with me, here, in this moment?"

Creating Distance

- "You were very close to your difficult inner experience for some breaths. Now, as you connect with your observer perspective, can you find some distance from the experience, as if taking a step back internally and looking at it?"

- “Please stay in the observer perspective for a few breaths. Notice how you are sitting here, doing this exercise. Notice your difficult inner experience with a bit more distance. Does that change anything for you? Maybe yes, maybe no—both are okay. We just want to observe.”

Returning to the Experience

- “After observing yourself for a few breaths, sitting here right now and doing this exercise, please come close again to your difficult inner experience, so that you can feel it in your body. Is it still in the same place as before? Does it feel the same or different?”
- “Take a few more breaths with the willingness to feel the inner experience, and continue to notice what happens.”

Reconnecting with Distance

- “Now, take some distance again and observe that you are sitting here, allowing your inner experience.”
- “Take as much time as you need to complete this exercise for yourself.”

Reflection and Feedback

- “How was that for you? Is there anything you would like to share?”

Key Points of the Exercise

- Empowerment through the observer perspective: Connecting with the observer perspective empowers the client by creating distance from the difficult experience.
- Fostering psychological flexibility: The client learns to move fluidly between sensing (self-as-process) and observing (self-as-context), fostering psychological flexibility.
- Client autonomy: Clients can pause or stop the exercise at any time if it becomes too overwhelming. They can resume when ready.

6.2.5 Exercise: Noticing and Distancing by Objectifying

The client in this exercise experiences multiple health issues, including chronic head pain, which, along with thoughts about it worsening, dominates her attention during work and leisure.

Exercise

Therapist: "What are you noticing right now?"

Client: "The pain in my head and the thoughts about what I should do."

Therapist: "How does the pain in your head feel right now?"

Client: "It's difficult to describe. It's a burning sensation, but also a pressure."

Therapist: "What else do you notice in your body?"

Client: "I feel helpless."

Therapist: "Where in your body do you feel the helplessness?"

Client: "In my stomach."

Therapist: "How does the helplessness feel in your stomach? Hard or soft, smooth or rough?"

Client: "It feels like a lump of wet clay in my stomach."

Therapist: "Can you imagine taking that lump of clay in your hands for a moment and shaping something from it?"

Client: "Yes, I can do that. I could form a bowl."

Therapist: "What does the bowl represent to you?"

Client: "Experiences. I can collect them in the bowl."

Therapist: "How about the experience of the headache? Can you collect that in the bowl as well?"

Client: "Yes, I can."

Therapist: "Who is noticing that you are doing this?"

Client: "I am noticing it."

Therapist: "Does this 'I' that notices have the pain, or does it observe the pain?"

Client: "It observes the pain."

Therapist: "Could you continue practicing this—observing all your experiences with the 'I' and collecting them in the bowl over the next few days?"

Client: "Yes, that sounds good."

Therapist: "Can you imagine putting the bowl back into your stomach?"

Variation 1

Client: "Yes, that works."

Therapist: "How do you feel your headache now? Did it become stronger, weaker, or stay the same during the exercise?"

Variation 2

Client: "No, I want to keep the bowl outside. I'd prefer to throw it against the wall."

Therapist: "Go ahead and try it. Do you recognize this? All the attempts to get rid of the pain?"

Client: "Oh yes, I'm familiar with that."

Therapist: "How well did that work for you?"

Client: "Well, it didn't work at all."

Therapist: "How about doing something different with it now? And just to check—whose pain is it? Whose bowl?"

Client: "My pain, my bowl."

Therapist: "So, it's a part of your experience, a part of you?"

Client: "Yes."

Therapist: "What happens when you keep rejecting parts of yourself?"

Client: "What?"

Therapist: "Could it be that you end up rejecting yourself and wondering, 'What's wrong with me? Who am I really, that I'm always carrying this pain?'"

Client: "Sounds familiar."

Therapist: "What do you think would happen if you accepted yourself as you are, with this pain?"

Key Points of the Exercise

- Broadening awareness: The client expanded her narrow focus on the headache to include other bodily and emotional experiences, such as different qualities of the pain, the feeling of helplessness, and related images.
- Integrating rejected feelings: Noticing the previously ignored sense of helplessness enabled the client to create a surprising new image—the bowl—for her difficult experience.

- Strengthening self-efficacy: Experimenting with the image fostered a sense of empowerment. The client learned that she could relate to her pain in different ways—whether by integrating it or by expressing frustration toward it.
- Defusing through objectification: By turning the sensation into an external object (the bowl), she moved from being fused with helplessness to observing it more distantly.
- Encouraging flexible perspective shifts: The instructions supported movement between self-as-process (sensing and feeling) and self-as-context (observing and integrating).
- Embracing uncertainty: There is no "wrong" outcome in an exercise. Trust your therapeutic intention, and stay open when the client's response surprises you.

6.2.6 **Metaphor:** River of Life

A metaphor I learned from my Sierra Leonean friend, Hannah Keittel Vonjoe, for the ever-changing nature of internal and external processes is the "River of Life." This metaphor beautifully illustrates how our stream of life flows continuously, with all its twists, turns, and challenges. It offers two perspectives: (1) you can focus on the self-as-process aspect, noticing and naming the ever-changing content of the present moment, or (2) you can emphasize the self-as-context aspect, recognizing that while the river's content changes, the river remains the same within its riverbed and flows toward its destination, the sea.

Metaphor

The river of life flows continuously, over rocks and tree trunks, home to fish and crocodiles. You can go with the flow of the river, or hold on to a rock and resist the current. Regardless of your actions, the river will keep flowing.

It's the same river from the source to the mouth, even though it constantly changes. There is only one direction or goal: the next river or, ultimately, the sea.

We can view ourselves as the entire river, or as the content within the river—the fish, the trees, and the water itself. Alternatively, we can also observe the river from the shore, which means we are not connected to the flow. Or we can see ourselves as the riverbed through which the river flows—connected to the content, yet separate from it. These perspectives are all valuable, and you can move between them, trying out what each one offers.

Key Points of the Metaphor

- Self-as-process: The river metaphor effectively represents self-as-process by showing how both pleasant and unpleasant experiences are part of life's ongoing flow.

- Embracing the flow: The metaphor encourages embracing the flow of life, suggesting that it might be more beneficial to go with the current than to fight against it. Giving up resistance can help conserve energy.
- Resistance and acceptance: The metaphor acknowledges that resistance is natural ("It's okay to resist"), but promotes acceptance by emphasizing that the river (life) will keep flowing anyway.
- Direction and meaning: The metaphor also suggests that there is a valuable direction—toward the sea—reminding one of the overarching, more meaningful directions in life.
- Self-as-context: The metaphor offers an understanding of self-as-context. Being the riverbed allows one to see oneself as connected to the content, yet distinct from it. This promotes the ability to step back and view experiences with greater perspective and flexibility.
- Fostering flexibility: Furthermore, moving between the different perspectives on the river fosters flexibility, as each one offers a different view of the same ongoing process.

6.2.7 Exercise: We-as-Process

A key goal of this exercise is cultivating flexibility in relationships, as our connection with ourselves is often challenged when interacting with others. With repeated practice, we can learn to stay connected to our own experiences, even while being present with another person.

In this exercise (from McHugh et al., 2019), two partners are taking turns, where each partner's perception evokes the next perception in the other. The goal is to remain aware of and present with the other person's experiences while staying connected to one's own.

Exercise

Turn to your partner and choose roles: A and B.

A begins by stating:	"I notice 'X' [e.g., a body sensation, feeling, or thought]."
B responds:	"This makes me think 'Y.'"
A replies:	"You saying that makes me feel 'Z.'"
B continues:	"As you say that, I notice the urge to 'X.'"

Repeat this exchange for a few minutes, noticing the effect of this exchange on both partners.

Key Points of the Exercise

- Awareness of context: The exercise encourages the client to notice how their experience changes depending on the context—the partner's responses.
- Challenging self-as-content: The exercise undermines the rigidity of self-as-content through current relationship-experience. By engaging with the partner, the client challenges the fixed nature of their identity and experience, allowing for more fluidity in how they relate to themself.
- Mutual influence: Engaging in real-time exchange highlights how both partners are shaping and being shaped by the interaction—each response stimulating new thoughts, feelings, and urges.

6.2.8 Recognizing Progress in Self-as-Process

As clients practice self-as-process, they may begin to notice changes in how they relate to their internal experiences:

- The client starts to name internal experiences that they previously perceived vaguely or couldn't articulate.
- The client remains present with themself even when the internal experiences are challenging or painful.
- The client begins to talk about their emotions in real time, for example: "I thought I didn't care, but I noticed how anxious I was during the job interview" or "I'm not comfortable with this exercise right now."

6.3 Flexibility with Self-as-Content

Self-as-content develops throughout our lives as verbal beings. When asked, "What makes you the person you are?" you can reflect and tell me. For example, I might say, "I am female, a clinical psychologist, European, happily married, tall, mostly friendly, open, curious, with a rather poor memory and self-doubts. I am who I am through my body, my movements, my language, and much more." This self-perception arises from learning language itself and from sensory experiences, feedback from others, comparison with others, and cultural learning.

We often think that we are "just the way we are," but we can always add something different. Each aspect of ourselves is subject to change—in the short term, in different situations, and in the long term, through development, learning, and life transitions, such as moving to another country or starting a new job. Some aspects of self-content are added intentionally, like learning a new language, playing an instrument, or pursuing something adventurous and unforeseen. Other aspects are imposed by life, such as coping with the pain of a divorce or learning that people can be hostile and harmful. Even desired life events force us to grow, such as becoming a parent or landing the challenging job of our dreams.

Clients often come to therapy when their self-image is shaken by difficult life events—losing a loved one, experiencing a sudden illness or accident, or being laid off from a job. Such profound changes can threaten the self-image, which may feel narrow and restrictive, yet also serve as a home and source of stability. Therefore, it's essential to explore how a person can engage with the different facets of their self-content in a flexible way. Which aspects support them in taking meaningful steps, and which ones may hinder effective action?

In most self-as-content exercises, the focus is on creating distance from self-content and adopting new perspectives, often overlapping with self-as-context practices. These exercises help clients recognize how they are entangled with their self-content and how this entanglement limits them. Through regular practice, they often become more able to accept the pain associated with difficult life events and may even discover new, enriching perspectives on their new situation.

6.3.1 Exercise: The Mango Tree

The "Mango Tree" exercise was developed during a workshop in Sierra Leone, West Africa, initiated by the workshop leader, Edmond Brandon. It is particularly useful for clients who feel stuck in a specific internal experience, such as frustration with a situation or relationship that seems unchangeable.

Exercise

Therapist: "Is it okay if we do an exercise about this?"

Client: [Nods.]

Therapist: "Let's stand up. Can you find a posture that expresses how constrained you feel in this situation with your mother?"

Client: [Assumes a rigid posture.]

Therapist: "Thank you. Now, please imagine you are a tree—maybe a mango tree. Picture a gentle wind starting to blow, moving you. The wind sways the mango tree back and forth. Let yourself move along with it. Start slow and take your time. Now, you can let the movement become larger if it feels right, including your arms. How does it feel to become more flexible, to expand, to try new movements?"

Client: [Moving.] "It feels more free, less tense."

Therapist: "When you think about how narrow you feel in the situation with your mother, does any new idea come to mind about what you could try? It sounds like your mother may not change her behavior, but is there anything you could do from your side?"

Client: "I feel sadness now. I think I've been pushing this sadness away all my life."

Therapist: "I'm glad you can feel this sadness and share it with me. Maybe nobody listened to you or helped you handle this sadness, so you didn't know what to do with it."

Client: "Nobody was ever interested in my feelings."

Therapist: "That's sad to hear." [Gives a moment of silence for the sadness to be felt.] "You know what? I am listening to you. I am interested in your feelings."

Client: "Yes, I can feel that."

Therapist: "How would it be to say to yourself: 'I listen to myself. I listen to my sadness.'"

Client: "I'm not sure. Will it help?"

Therapist: "I can't promise it will. But as nobody ever did that for you, it might be something new to try. For me, it seems like this sadness wants to be heard. Would you be willing to give it a try?"

Key Points of the Exercise

- Physical expression: The client physically expresses their emotional constraint, creating a direct connection between their body and inner experience.
- External movement inspires inner movement: The metaphor of the swaying mango tree introduces gentle flexibility, offering a soft way to approach a rigid, difficult experience.
- Exploring feelings: The exercise helps the client connect with and explore feelings they previously avoided.
- Fostering ownership and self-efficacy: By introducing the idea of self-listening, the exercise teaches the client that they can offer themself what was missing earlier in their life.
- Broader therapeutic goals: The exercise creates a platform for moving toward acceptance, exploring values, or addressing other therapeutic goals based on the situation.

6.3.2 Exercise: Left Foot–Right Foot

This exercise almost always produces remarkable results, likely because acceptance, values, and commitment are put into motion experientially, naturally leading to the observer perspective. I like to use it when clients feel stuck in their self-content, as they can gain clarity about what is truly valuable to them, what steps they wish to take, and also where they may not yet feel ready to act.

Exercise

Invite your client to stand beside you in the therapy room, their back against a wall from which they can take a few steps forward.

Setting the Direction

Therapist: "You mentioned that you feel stuck in your upset with your partner. Now, imagine you're looking toward the direction that represents what you truly want in your relationship in the long term. Please decide where that is—for example, toward the plant, the golden lamp, or something else in the room."

Client: "Toward the golden lamp."

Therapist: "Wonderful, that's the direction you want to go. While my room ends there, in your life, this direction extends much further. What name would you give this direction that is valuable for you?"

Client: "Having a loving relationship with my partner."

Acknowledging the Current Reality

Therapist: "Very good. Now, here you are, standing where you are today. As you mentioned, you had a strong argument with your partner, which happens often. Are you ready to stand here, acknowledging that you feel stuck in your upset with your partner, while you desire to have a loving relationship?"

Option 1: Acceptance:

Client: "It's not easy, but yes."

Therapist: "Great. Please move your left foot forward, and we'll call this your 'acceptance step.' By accepting where you are—acknowledging that you're upset with your partner—you've taken a step toward your valuable direction. Do you notice any difference after taking this step?"

Client: "Yes, I feel more stable like this."

Option 2: Resistance:

Client: "No, I don't want to be here."

Therapist: "That's fine. You're not ready to stand where you are, being upset with your partner. And yet, you are in this situation. How does that feel?"

Client: "I feel even more stuck. It's hopeless."

Therapist: "Thank you for noticing and sharing that. That is very helpful. Are you willing to accept that you don't agree with being where you are, feeling stuck and hopeless?"

Client: [Nods.]

Therapist: "Thank you. This means you are taking one important step, to be where you are right now. To accept that you are not willing to be where you are, feeling stuck and hopeless, being upset with your partner. Let's move the left foot forward to take this step."

Client: [Moves left foot forward.]

Therapist: "Do you notice any difference after taking this step?"

Client: "Hmm, somehow it feels more real now."

Exploring Actions

Therapist: "Now, from here, looking toward your valuable direction, does any action come to mind that you'd like to take, maybe now or after the session?"

Client: "I think I want to have a conversation with my partner."

Therapist: "Great. Is there anything specific you'd like to say?"

Client: "I'd like to apologize for being mean during our last fight."

Therapist: "Wonderful step. Let's take it together symbolically by moving our right foot forward. We'll call this the 'commitment step.' Does it feel right to take this step?"

Client: [Moves right foot forward.] "Yes, it feels good. It goes in the right direction."

Accepting Consequences

Therapist: "Now, an important question: You're taking this step with the intention of moving toward a loving relationship with your partner. However, you don't know how this action will turn out. Your partner may engage with you, or not; the conversation may go as you hope, or it may not. Are you ready to accept the possible outcomes?"

Client: "Yes, that's okay. I don't know how it will go, but I want to try."

Therapist: "Let's now move your left foot forward again for another acceptance step, allowing the possible consequences."

This second acceptance step is crucial, as it offers the client a choice by confronting possible failures, helping maintain motivation even in the face of setbacks. When anticipated and already accepted, setbacks lose much of their power to intimidate. In case the client is not willing to face the potential consequences, I would assume the step is too large and look for a smaller, more manageable step they are willing to explore. Depending on the client's readiness, you may stop here or explore one or two additional committed actions.

Key Points of the Exercise

- Fostering flexibility with rigid self-content: Simply getting up from the chair fosters more flexibility; clients get in touch with themselves and come up with ideas they didn't have while sitting. This is my frequent observation.
- Contacting all self processes: The exercise touches upon all self processes: self-as-process (e.g. perceiving and naming willingness or resistance, doing something new), acceptance and distancing from self-as-content (e.g., "I'm in an argument again," "I see no way out," "I allow it," "I take a conscious step"), and self-as-context (taking different perspectives on oneself, such as "I-here-now," "I-at home-later," the values perspective, "I notice myself doing that step").

6.3.3 Exercise: Fun with Self-Content

You can use the following exercise in a one-on-one session, but it works particularly well in groups, which is where I developed it. It's a dynamic activity, and most participants find it refreshing and enjoyable. In a one-on-one session, you can decide whether to participate with the client or simply guide them through the exercise.

Exercise

In a group setting, ask the group:

"Please find a partner and decide who will respond to the questions first. I will ask you to share different types of stories about yourself. You'll have one minute for each story before switching roles."

1. "What is a story you like to tell about yourself?"
   Share your story with your partner, then switch roles.
2. "What is a story you feel a little uncomfortable telling about yourself?"
   Share your story with your partner, then switch roles.
3. "What is a story about you that is completely fictitious and absurd?"
   Share your story with your partner, then switch roles.
4. "What is a story about you that is made up but would be really cool if it came true?"
   Share your story with your partner, then switch roles.

Debrief

- How was that experience?
- What did you notice?
- How do you feel now?
- Do you have more or less distance from yourself?

Key Points of the Exercise

- Sharing the self: Encourages the sharing of positive, challenging, and nonsensical aspects of the self to cultivate more freedom with self-knowledge.
- Practicing perspective-taking: Introduces perspective shifts such as truth, fiction, absurdity, and possibility, helping participants gain distance from self-content.
- New possibilities: The fourth question playfully invites the creation of new possibilities.

6.3.4 Exploring the Function of Self-as-Content

Use the following questions to increase awareness and explore the function of persistent self-content:

- "This feeling of anger arises quite often. It seems to be important to you. What is it about? What does it tell you? Does it help you with something (e.g., expressing limits, realizing that something is not okay)?"
- "You've mentioned spending a lot of time ruminating on this issue and that you'd like to quit your job. Could there be something important about the rumination? Might it serve a purpose (e.g., finding a solution, avoiding certain feelings, etc.)?"
- "What action does this thought about what could go wrong for your child suggest to you right now? What would the result of that action be? Is it aligned with what you want in the long term?"
- "Is it important for you to follow this rule, or is it important for others that you follow it?"

KEY POINTS OF THE QUESTIONS

- Awareness and distance: Asking these questions increases the client's awareness of pressing self-content and fosters distance from it.
- Understanding function: Exploring the function of difficult self-content can broaden the client's perspective and reveal more helpful ways to address their underlying needs or yearnings.

6.3.5 Recognizing Progress with Self-as-Content

- Observed behavior changes in session: The client can now allow difficult thoughts or feelings, observe them with some distance, and even bring humor to the experience. Or a client shares their successes for the first time, rather than focusing solely on what they didn't achieve.

- Changes reported by clients in daily life: A client who previously experienced regular binge eating episodes when alone in their apartment now finds comfort in sitting on the sofa, cuddling up in a blanket, and drinking tea, even enjoying time alone.
- Development of valuable rules: "Whenever this fear comes up, I pause, breathe, allow it for a moment, and then return to what I want to do." Or: "When I wake up feeling depressed, I do this noticing exercise, so I don't get entangled in harmful behaviors anymore."
- Revisions of self-labels: "Actually, this diagnosis I once gave myself annoys me now. I'm not a narcissist, and I don't have to behave that way."

6.4 Deriving Self-as-Context

We've established that self-as-context has two major aspects:

1. Perspective-taking: Recognizing that one experiences everything from the viewpoint of "I-here-now," and that everybody else has their own point of view; applying deictic relations such as "I am here," "you are there," and "something is happening now or then," to objects, persons, thoughts, feelings, bodily experiences, or roles.
2. Hierarchical perspective: A broader, overarching awareness from which a person can include any content as part of themself while recognizing that they are more than that content. The hierarchical perspective helps integrate elements such as values, purpose, kindness, and compassion.

Practicing self-as-context involves exploring various perspectives with your clients. For example:

- Having clients reflect on their past, present, or future experiences, or aspects of their self.
- Having clients reflect on their inner and outer behavior and their roles in different situations.
- Having clients imagine viewing their behavior from someone else's perspective, such as a best friend or wiser self.
- Having clients physically take different spatial perspectives within the therapy room.

These exercises help clients adopt a broader, more flexible perspective on themselves. This enables them to look at distressing or restrictive content with greater distance and kindness, and consciously align their actions with their values and desires.

Ultimately, self-as-context emerges from practicing multiple perspectives, providing space for more creative thinking, open feeling, and purposeful acting. The overarching goal is to support individuals in cultivating the freedom to express themselves and to act in flexible, sustainable, meaningful ways, while staying aware of their given context.

Be aware that using the observer perspective to promote self-as-context may activate an inner critical voice, and clients might confuse the two. When you hear comments like, "I can notice that I'm sitting here, feeling this emotion, and I don't like what I see. It's the same old me," you can guide the client one step further. You can ask, "And who is noticing that you don't like what you see?" to help the client move beyond the critical voice and connect to the neutral observer perspective.

Fostering the client's connection with their actual, direct experiences—which involves practicing self-as-process—is key in all self-as-context exercises. Self-as-context is not about abstract or purely verbal knowledge, but is grounded in immediate, embodied experiences.

Dare to experiment with the exercises described below. Start by trying them yourself, with friends, and finally with your clients. My way to do them might not be the best way for you, as we are all have our own styles as therapists. Always remain mindful of the exercise's intention for each specific client and moment. As your understanding of the exercises deepens, you'll gain clarity about their function and be able to adapt or invent exercises tailored to the unique themes and contexts of your clients.

6.4.1 Exercise: Practicing Autonomy and Choice

This exercise is a great way to begin a session, especially when your clients—or even you—are feeling distressed. You can apply it after your clients have had some practice with perspective-taking, helping them explore what truly matters to them. It works best with eyes closed or focused on a spot that does not distract the person. Make sure to give the client some space between the prompts to experience each sentence.

Exercise

- "Take a moment to notice yourself and realize that you are sitting here in this room, hearing my voice. Be aware of your body, feel it touching the chair, notice your feet on the ground or wherever they are."
- "Notice that you, this person you call 'I,' is present in your body, right here, right now."
- "Be aware that you moved your body here today because you wanted to be here. Notice that you are an autonomous human being. You could decide to stand up and go, right here, right now."
- "Something must be valuable to you, given that you are here. Notice what that is."
- "Notice again that your 'I' is present in your body and that you are the only person present within your body. Nobody else could live in your body, just you. You have been living in this body since you were born."

- "Notice that it is your one and only body—no second version is available. A precious thing, and worth being treated with care. Your body allows you to be present right here, right now. Maybe you would like to take a moment to thank your body and to listen to it, to see if something wants to be noticed."

[Pause briefly to allow reflection.]

- "Please be aware that you perceive your body from your 'I,' which is present right here, right now. Your 'I' can feel your body, and your 'I' can notice that you are doing that."
- "It is also your 'I' that is hearing my voice right here, right now."
- "Your 'I' hears my voice and can notice that you are hearing it."
- "Your 'I' is doing this exercise right here, right now. And your 'I' can notice that you are doing this exercise with me."
- "So, from your 'I-here-now,' you can perceive yourself, and you can look at yourself—feeling your body, hearing my voice, and doing this exercise. We could call this the observer perspective."
- "Is there anything specific or new that you notice from this observer perspective?"

[Pause briefly to allow reflection.]

- "Please conclude the exercise for yourself and come back to our shared space."
- "How was that experience for you? Is there anything you would like to share from the exercise? What would be valuable for you here today?"

Key Points of the Exercise

- Raising awareness: The connection to the body and the present moment becomes more conscious, as does the free choice and the value to be present.
- Practice observing: Perceiving and observing the perceiving are emphasized and differentiated.
- Perspective-taking: The perspective of "I-here-now" is strengthened, and the observer perspective is introduced.

6.4.2 Exercise: Observer on a Flipchart Paper

The original version of this exercise comes from my long-term supervisor, Rainer Sonntag. I use this exercise with individuals and couples as a way to step out of the therapy chair and encourage new perspectives.

Exercise

Begin by placing a blank sheet of flip chart paper on the floor, and invite the client to stand in the middle of it. Ask them to imagine the paper as their "Self," expanding in all directions, encompassing everything they know about themself, as well as additional possibilities. You can then invite them to write down how they see themself at that moment—what they believe defines their self.

Allow a few minutes for writing.

Once they've written down the aspects they consider most important, ask them to stand on the paper again and look at it from above. You can guide their reflection with questions like:

- "How does it feel to look at yourself from this perspective?"
- "What is it like to be this person?"
- "Can you give space to everything you've written, or is there something you find disruptive?"

For example, one client remarked, "I only wrote down positive aspects. Nobody likes to admit negative traits."

I responded, "What about you? What would you like to do with the aspects you find negative?"

After reflecting, she said, "Write them down." She wrote those aspects down, and when she stood on the flip chart again, she said, "It feels more whole now." You could clearly observe the expansion and acceptance this brought.

Exploring Further

There are many playful ways to deepen the exercise. For example, you can strike out certain self-aspects and ask, "If I take this away, is that still you?" If the client responds, "That's not me anymore," follow up with, "If this is not you, then who is it?"

These explorations often reveal that the person remains the same human being, no matter the changes in their self-content. While some possibilities may not be realistic (such as becoming a prima ballerina at seventy, or a math genius when you prefer hands-on work), many others remain available.

One client, for example, wrote down all the "contradictory" things about himself. He described being a "loving father" to his young son while simultaneously "fearing having another child." He wrote that he "loves playing with his son" but also "misses the freedom to travel the world" and feels a "longing" for that time. Seeing these aspects side by side on the paper resolved the tension for him. He later felt more at ease discussing the idea of having a second child with his wife.

Application in Couples Therapy

In couples therapy, I let both partners write down their "Self" on their own flip chart, without peeping at the other one.

Then I ask additional questions, such as:

- "What do you see when you look from your place to your partner's self?"
- I invite them to switch places: "Would you like to stand in your partner's place? What is it like to be them? What do you see from there when you look back at your own place?"
- Another step might be: "Would you like to add something or take something away from your partner's self?" and I ask the partner, "How does that feel for you now?"

Key Points of the Exercise

- The continuity of self: No matter what is added or removed, the person remains the same. A person has multiple possibilities for changing or expanding their behaviors while staying true to themself.
- Integration and acceptance: This exercise allows space for all aspects of the self, including resistance and contradictions, which often dissolve naturally. Acceptance frequently emerges from the observer perspective, standing on the flipchart paper.
- Awareness of self-view: Clients notice the tone of how they view themselves—whether it's critical, deprecating, or loving—and realize that they have the choice to bring more kindness and compassion into their view.
- Perspective-taking in couples: In the couples' version, this exercise fosters mutual understanding and playfulness. It allows partners to gain new perspectives and often discover that their partner's view of them is more loving and enriching than they assumed.

6.4.3 Exercise: I-Here-Now

This is a complex exercise that I find quite powerful and use a lot to foster perspective-taking and contact with I-here-now. Rainer Sonntag introduced this exercise in a training for ACT trainers years ago. It can be confusing at first. You can practice the deictic perspectives of "I" vs. "you," "here" vs. "there," and "now" vs. "then" using simple objects, from which the observer perspective can naturally emerge. Some clients grasp this quickly, while others struggle, and you may notice that a more distant relationship to their self-content is an issue for the clients who struggle.

Exercise: Part 1

Therapist: "An exercise comes to mind that could be helpful for you. It might feel a little funny. Are you okay with that?"

Client: "Yes, let's try."

Therapist: "Great. We'll start simple. Please choose an arbitrary object in the room and tell me which one."

Client: "The bouquet on the table."

Therapist: "The bouquet on the table, very good. You can see the bouquet, and you can also see that there is a distance between you and the bouquet. You and the bouquet are two different things, right?"

Client: "Yes, that's true."

Therapist: "Good. And who perceives the bouquet?"

Client: "I perceive it."

Therapist: "Very good. And your 'I' that perceives the bouquet, where is this 'I' from your point of view? Would you say it is 'here' or 'there'?" [Point to "here" and "there."]

Client: "Hmm, I am here."

Therapist: "Great. And the bouquet, from your point of view, is it 'here' or 'there'?" [Point again.]

Client: "The bouquet is there."

Therapist: "Very good. And when do you notice that?"

Client: "When I look at it. Now."

Therapist: "Great. Can we practice this with another object? Please choose one."

Client: "The globe on the shelf."

Therapist: "Thanks. And who is perceiving the globe?"

Client: "I perceive the globe."

Therapist: "Great. And the globe, from your point of view, is it 'here' or 'there'?" [Point to "here" and "there."]

Client: "The globe is there."

Therapist: "Very good. And your 'I' that perceives the globe, is it 'here' or 'there' from your point of view?" [Point to "here" and "there."]

Client: "I am here."

Therapist: "Good. And again, there is a distance between you and the globe, right, you are not the same thing? Do you also notice that you establish a connection with the globe, when you perceive it?"

Client: "That's right, I have not really noticed the globe before."

[Repeat the same process with the new object, and one or two others if necessary. Most clients will begin to notice similarities and differences in their perceptions. You can add the point about distance and connection at any time. This one is important, as self-as-context is not about separating, but about flexibility with connecting and distancing.]

Therapist: "We've done this a few times. Do you notice what stays the same and what changes?"

Client: "Yes, 'I' always perceive the objects. I perceive them 'now' and from 'here.' The objects change."

Therapist: "Excellent. Now I have a question: Could you perceive anything at another time than 'now'?"

Client: "Hmm, I could imagine things at another time."

Therapist: "That's right, you can imagine anything, at any time. But is that the same as perceiving? Can you perceive things at another time than 'now'?"

Client: "No, I can only perceive now."

Therapist: "Exactly. And can you be anywhere other than 'here'?"

Client: "No, not really."

Therapist: "And when you're on the street after the session, where are you then, from your point of view?"

Client: "I am also 'here,' even when I'm out on the street."

Therapist: "Great. And can you look from anywhere other than 'I'?"

Client: "No, I can't. I can only look from 'I,' from myself."

With this part of the exercise, you establish the perspective of "I-here-now" and make it experiential for the client. The content changes, but "I-here-now" is constant.

You can extend the exercise to thoughts and feelings either immediately or in a future session. The process works in a similar way. However, most clients perceive thoughts and feelings as "here" rather than "there," unlike objects such as the bouquet or the globe. This lack of perceived distance is precisely what makes dealing with thoughts and feelings more challenging.

Additionally, you can invite the client to use you, the therapist, as the object and practice "I-here-now" in relation to another person. This variation can be particularly helpful for clients who feel entangled in their personal relationships.

Exercise: Part 2

Therapist: "Can you tell me a thought you're noticing right now?"

Client: "Yes, that I hate myself for my outbursts with my kids."

Therapist: "Thank you. Who is noticing this thought, that you hate yourself for your outbursts with your kids?"

Client: "I am noticing the thought."

Therapist: "And where do you notice the thought? Is it 'here' or maybe 'there'?" [Again, point to "here" and "there."]

Client: "The thought is definitely here, in my head."

Therapist: "Good. Can you notice that you are sitting here, doing this exercise with me?"

Client: "Yes, I can notice that."

Therapist: "Good. You can sit here, and you can look at yourself sitting here, right? We called this the observer perspective earlier. And the observer perspective—do you experience it as 'here' or 'there'?"

Client: "For me the observer is 'there.'"

Therapist: "Great. So, you experience the observer 'there,' and the observer can perceive your 'I' sitting here, having this thought. From the observer perspective, where is your thought?"

Client: "Hmm. From the observer perspective, the thought is 'there.'"

Therapist: "Okay. So, from the perspective of the observer, do you have more distance or less distance to your thought?"

Client: "I have more distance."

Therapist: "Okay. And is it still your thought, is it connected to you?"

Client: "Definitely, it is still part of me."

Therapist: "Great. Is that helpful in any way?"

Typically, it is helpful for the client to gain distance and to experience a choice—the choice of how to look at a thought or feeling, and how to deal with it. However, the conversation can unfold differently. You need to stick to your purpose, for example practicing noticing, practicing the different perspectives, practicing distance and connection. It's meant to be an exploratory process, requiring flexibility and practice on the therapist's part. Many clients enjoy this exercise and apply it in different situations outside the therapy room, with objects or even with people they feel entangled with.

I'd like to mention that the observer perspective—looking at oneself—is an adaptation of mine. Rainer Sonntag himself prefers the perspective of viewing objects, thoughts, and emotions from the "I-here-now" standpoint, in order to avoid potential unwanted side effects, such as unhelpful dissociation.

So far, I haven't encountered such side effects in my work, though that may also depend on the client population. I value his simpler approach and continue to explore both variations in practice. I invite you to do the same.

Key Points of the Exercise

- Cultivating a distant perspective: The distant perspective is cultivated by viewing various examples of objects from the "I-here-now" standpoint. Since all the objects are physically present in the room, this approach feels tangible and concrete.
- Extending to thoughts and feelings: Extending this practice to thoughts and feelings is straightforward and often insightful for clients. They can apply the distant perspective they developed with objects, allowing them to observe their thoughts and feelings rather than being immersed in them or having their perception restricted by them.
- Balancing distance and connection: Through this process, clients come to experience themselves as both distanced from and connected to external objects, as well as to their own thoughts and feelings.
- Flexibly shifting perspectives: Clients practice shifting flexibly between a distant perspective and a more hierarchical observer perspective (e.g., "I am having this thought" vs. "This thought is part of me"), expanding their ability to relate to internal content in multiple helpful ways.

6.4.4 Other-as-Context in Conversation

By providing our clients with a nonjudgmental space, we offer them an experience of other-as-context, allowing them to learn—through our model—to create a more flexible context for themselves. This happens continuously in conversation, and at times, we can intentionally use a dialogue to highlight other-as-context.

CASE EXAMPLE

An overweight patient shares her food diary with me. She's a young bus driver, full of humor and positivity, despite her challenging life circumstances. We laugh a lot in the sessions. She decided on her own to track her food intake and share it with me. I thank her for her trust and begin reading parts of the diary aloud so she can participate in the process. At one point, I acknowledge: "Wow, this is quite a lot of ice cream, pizza, chocolate, and chips you're eating daily." She averts her gaze and admits to feel ashamed since writing down the numerous entries. I gently ask if she would feel okay looking at me. After some reflection, she turns her head to meet my gaze.

OPTION 1

Therapist: "When you see me looking at you, do you see anything that increases your shame?"

Client: "No, nothing. I see kindness and neutrality. It's strange—I can't even put it into words."

Therapist: "Where words fail us, it usually gets interesting. Please notice how it feels. What's so strange?"

Client: "Hmmm. It's strange not to be judged. To be honest, I don't know what to do with my self-pity now."

[The client smiles, finding some humor in her words.]

In the following session, she shares that my neutrality and kindness helped her cultivate more self-compassion (instead of self-pity), leading to healthier eating habits and reduced consumption of processed foods.

OPTION 2

Therapist: "When you see me looking at you, do you notice anything that increases your shame?"

Client: "Yes, I feel very ashamed, seeing you looking at me."

Therapist: "Thank you for sharing that. It must be very difficult for you to bear this deep shame. Would it be okay to allow the shame here in between us for a few breaths?"

Client: "Somehow, it's relieving to allow the shame to just be there. Normally I push it away, but honestly, it's always there. I'm constantly wondering what others think of me—my body, my weight. I even think you might worry about the sofa breaking when I sit on it."

KEY POINTS OF THE CONVERSATION

- Facing shame: Being courageous and bringing the feeling of shame into the immediate conversation allows the client to confront and process it directly.
- Self-compassion and acceptance: In option 1, the client becomes aware of her self-pity, leading to self-compassion (this is how it went with that client). In option 2, the client allows shame to exist in the therapeutic relationship, learning to accept it rather than suppress it.
- Modeling compassion: By embodying nonjudgment and compassion, we as therapists provide a model for our clients to create the same kind of compassionate context for themselves.

6.4.5 Perspective over Time

When a client shares a difficult experience, such as saying, "I feel very insecure," you can use this moment to practice the observer perspective. Together, you can explore other situations where they've felt similarly, encouraging reflection on patterns and recurring themes. This approach often helps clients create emotional distance and allows them to better understand their own history.

Therapist: "You say you feel very insecure. Thanks for sharing that with me. Can you feel this insecurity in your body?"

Client: "Yes, I can feel it here in my stomach."

Therapist: "I am glad that you can feel it so clearly. And can you notice yourself, sitting here right now, feeling the insecurity in your stomach, telling that to me?"

Client: "Yes, I can notice that."

Therapist: "Good. So, we could say that you can observe yourself, as you sit here, feeling insecure. And this observer perspective, do you experience it more as looking at your experiences from the inside or looking at yourself from the outside of your body?"

Client: "I would say I'm looking more from the outside."

[In my experience, most clients see themselves from the outside, though sometimes also from the inside. Both perspectives can be valuable. This mirrors the distinction I mentioned earlier in Exercise 6.4.3. We can guide clients to observe thoughts, feelings, actions, and objects from the perspective of 'I-here-now'—as if standing "behind the camera," watching as experiences unfold. And we can additionally ask them to observe themselves as they engage in these thoughts, feelings and actions—stepping "in front of the camera," and seeing themselves through the lens of the observer.]

Therapist: "When you now see yourself, sitting here in my practice with this feeling, and when you use your observer perspective to go back in your memory, are there maybe earlier events in your life when this insecurity was also present? Do any situations come to your mind? Please give yourself a little time. You don't have to force it, just allow situations that fit to come up."

Client: "Yes, there was a situation at work recently."

Therapist: "Can you remember what you experienced in that situation? What happened before you started to feel insecure, and what did you do then?"

[You can continue to investigate diverse earlier situations with the client.]

When you explore situations where important feelings showed up, oftentimes clients start to remember other situations from their youth or childhood, maybe when those feelings first started. There is no need to force this, but if it comes up, that can be a great opportunity to bring new perspectives to the situation. For example, you can ask the client what they would like to give to their younger self when they look at this younger version of themself now, with their adult capacities.

They can imagine bringing their adult self to their younger self and offering help. They can imagine giving their younger self what they would have needed then, but didn't get at the time. Clients often experience this as healing and precious, giving them deeper access to acceptance. It is often easier to accept a child feeling insecure (or other vulnerable feelings) rather than an adult. It can become a beneficial habit for regulating emotions, to not immediately react to difficult feelings when they show up, but to take care of the younger self instead. Then the adult self can make adult decisions again.

6.4.6 Exercise: Self-as-Context in the Mirror

This is an exercise that I use with clients to help them develop a kinder and more compassionate view on themselves. I look into a mirror together with them and invite them to find a supportive sentence that resonates with them. This could mean saying to themselves in the mirror something like:

- "I love you, and I see your beauty."
- "I love you, and I trust that you're taking the right steps."
- Or even something playful like, "Good morning, sweetie."

This exercise is a practical way of helping clients connect with themselves in their daily life and offering them the unconditional love they deserve. It often feels strange for them at first, but I tell them that it is not about "believing" what they say or talking themselves into something. Instead, it is about adopting a supportive stance, like "Whatever I think or feel about myself, my stance is to accept and love me." To build this attitude, it initially helps to practice with every glance in the mirror. Over time, it can become something they do naturally, whenever it comes to mind.

Key Points of the Exercise

- Disrupt negative patterns: This practice interrupts harmful, judgmental self-talk and prevents clients from reinforcing unhelpful patterns, such as feeling bad about oneself, judging oneself in the mirror, and spiraling into negative emotions.
- Foster safety: It encourages independence from external validation and fosters a sense of safety and acceptance within oneself.

6.4.7 Metaphors for Self-as-Context

You can draw metaphors for self-as-context from everyday life:

On my way to a vacation, I was stuck in a big traffic jam with my husband. It was hot, I was tired and annoyed, and we still had hours of driving ahead. Other drivers were equally irritated, making reckless overtaking maneuvers, thus worsening the situation. In a sudden moment of awareness, I thought, "This is all part of my context." The traffic jam, along with all the frustrated people, became part of my self-as-context. In that moment, my annoyance disappeared. It was just as it was—neutral. This was a profound and memorable experience for me.

So, be creative and draw on whatever is part of your or your client's context—particularly things they love or places where they feel at home and can return to more often. Here are some examples:

CHRYSALIS AND BUTTERFLY

Self-as-context is like the chrysalis for the caterpillar: It provides a safe space and allows the caterpillar to patiently transform into a butterfly. The same molecules that formed the caterpillar now create the butterfly. It is the same, yet different. The butterfly struggles to emerge from the chrysalis. The butterfly is not "better" than the caterpillar; without the caterpillar, there would be no butterfly. Yet the butterfly has new perspectives and ways of moving through the world.

TWO WINGS: BEING SEEN AND LOVED

Being seen and being loved are like two wings, and we need both wings to fly. One wing is being loved—when we feel loved but not seen, it feels incomplete, as if the love isn't truly for us. The second wing is being seen—when we are seen but not loved, it can feel like being a speared butterfly. When we feel both loved and seen, we have two wings to fly (Brach, 2013).

WATER METAPHOR

Imagine sliding into the water of a lake or sea at the perfect temperature. The water welcomes you exactly as you are. It doesn't expect you to be any different. The water carries you and allows unlimited freedom of movement—there is no judgment, only liveliness. Practicing self-as-context means recognizing that you are both the water—vast, open, and accepting—and the person who slides into it.

UNIQUE PERSPECTIVE

While swimming with your face just above the water, you see the world like a hemisphere. It's your unique point of view, and it is the only one you can have. Every person looks from their unique "I-here-now." If you were not there, your distinct perspective on the world would be missing.

FOREST METAPHOR

Self-as-context is like entering a lush, green forest. It embraces you, offering a canopy of safety where you can confide your burdens to the trees. The forest absorbs everything, giving you a profound sense of security.

VARYING THE NOTICING PLACE

You can explore different perspectives with clients, helping them examine the vantage point from where they view themselves or life. For instance, in the observer exercise by Hayes, Strosahl, and Wilson (2004, p. 203), there's the "place behind your eyes." Or, as in the beautiful tale of friendship and relationships *The Little Prince*, we find that "One sees clearly only with the heart. What is essential is invisible to the eye." (de Saint-Exupéry, 1989). In the wisdom of the Sweet Medicine SunDance Path, a shamanic tradition for spiritual evolution mainly from the Americas, one can adopt the perspective from the "one-point," the center of the body located below the navel, which offers a view free from emotions. Many other traditions also provide gateways to what we call "self-as-context" in ACT.

BALD EAGLE METAPHOR

A metaphor that helped me during a challenging time, when I was confronted with disrespect and a lack of communication in my close environment, was an image I dreamed of at that time: a bald eagle sitting across from me, stretching its head toward the sun. The eagle kept its head high, turned toward the light, and refused to be pulled down. This image helped me stay connected to my values, even when I felt like becoming furious and mean.

MUSIC AS A METAPHOR

Music that reaches and includes everyone in a room can also be a powerful metaphor for self-as-context—especially for clients who have a strong connection to music.

Key Points of the Metaphors

- Multiple points of access: Metaphors reflect and provide access to critical aspects of self-as-context:
  - Creating space for everything present
  - Accepting, trusting, and even loving what is there when possible
  - Connecting to the whole, complete, and indestructible aspect of oneself
  - Offering a place of freedom and valuable choice
  - Allowing self-compassion
  - Opening the door to transcendence, spirituality, and vision in the client's worldview
- Pathways for growth: Metaphors allow clients to stay present with difficult content, feel safe within their context, and envision pathways for transformation and growth.

6.4.8 Questions to Foster Self-as-Context

It's powerful to weave self-as-context prompts into your conversations with clients. Doing so helps solidify the insights they've gained from exercises or metaphors, and supports them in applying their capacity for self-as-context across a variety of situations.

- Incorporate I-here-now/you-there-then perspectives: "Who is noticing this feeling right now?" or "How did you handle this when it happened then?" or "How would a person you admire deal with this problem?"
- Incorporate the hierarchical perspective: "Given that your thoughts, feelings, bodily experiences, and actions are parts of you—but that you are much more than just those—does anything new come to mind?"
- Incorporate the values perspective: "When you view yourself from the observer perspective, gaining some distance from your difficult thoughts and feelings, what valuable choice might you make?"

- Incorporate temporal perspectives: "Imagine looking back on this difficult decision thirty years from now—how might you evaluate it then? What would you be glad about? How would you have liked to act from that perspective?"
- Incorporate compassion: "Can you bring kindness and compassion to yourself as you observe yourself sitting here with this difficult feeling, such as, 'Wow, this really isn't easy for me?'"
- Incorporate others' perspectives: "What would your best friend say to you about this issue?" or "What advice would you give to your child if they asked you this question?" or "How does this marital conflict look from your husband's perspective, do you think?"
- Incorporate spatial perspectives: "If you were observing this problem from a mountaintop or a space shuttle, would it appear differently?" or "Looking at yourself from the other side of the room, what do you see?"
- Incorporate the relationship perspective in the moment: "When you look at me right now, what do you see? And what would you say I see when I look at you?"

Key Points of the Questions

- Perspective-taking: Encouraging connection with multiple perspectives to create distance from difficult content, while staying engaged with it as part of oneself.
- Inner stability: Fostering an experience of stability within the self, independent of specific content.
- Hierarchical perspective: Introducing overarching perspectives, like compassion or values, that can guide integration and stabilize the self.

6.4.9 Recognizing Progress with Self-as-Context

It's a joy to witness self-as-context capacities emerging in my clients. Our conversations become lighter and more connected, with greater mutual understanding. I can sense more clearly what they are expressing and reach them more easily, and they, in turn, gain a deeper understanding of both what I am saying and what they truly want. Some good indicators of this shift include:

- Humor arises more frequently in conversations and exercises for both you and your clients.
- Clients begin to describe the complexity of their experiences and adopt flexible perspectives. For example: "I was terribly afraid to take the elevator and wanted to use the stairs. Then I thought, 'Wait a minute, if my little son were here, what would I want him to learn from me?' So, I took the elevator."
- Clients find their own unique expressions of self-as-context, such as: "I imagine sitting on top of my wardrobe, looking down at the situation."
- Clients notice they can act independently of their feelings and even have positive experiences despite them: "I felt bad, ugly, and unlovable, but I decided to go to the party anyway. My friends were really happy to see me."

- Growing empathy for others: "In the past, I would've been so annoyed when that old man at the supermarket checkout counted out all his change. But this time, I felt touched by how hard it seemed for him. I even asked if I could help. He was pretty grumpy, but I was still glad I did it. Someday, I might be old, too."
- Clients may also receive novel feedback from important others, such as, "I feel like you understand me better now."
- Clients' actions increasingly align with their values.
- Self-compassion emerges naturally.
- You, as the therapist, find yourself learning from your clients more often.

6.5 Keeping Up New Behaviors

It's exciting to observe the progress of clients. The next step involves maintaining that progress and building effective structures for ongoing, conscious practice.

The experience of self-as-context begins to emerge through multiple examples of different perspectives on the continuous process of the self, combined with references to a broader, hierarchical perspective that observes the content. Over time, the "I-here-now" perspective can be recognized as a constant because it is the only element that never changes.

ESTABLISHING STRUCTURES FOR PRACTICE

Simple structures can help clients stick with the practice of connecting to self-as-context. These structures should be easy to follow and fit into everyday life, such as:

Morning routines—starting the day with short, intentional practices like:

- Staying in bed a little longer to recall plans for the day while reflecting on what matters and what one intends to hold as important.
- Taking ten mindful breaths at an open window while noting something to be thankful for.
- Sitting briefly on the edge of the bed to check in: "How am I today? Is there anything that wants to be noticed? What do I need? What's important to me today?"
- Taking a moment after arriving at work to pause and reflect on what feels important that day.

The core idea is to pause before diving into the day—connecting with oneself and setting a focus. These brief moments encourage self-awareness, foster self-as-process, create distance from content, and align actions with values. They build self-efficacy and strengthen a sense of ownership over the day.

During the day:

- It can be helpful to occasionally pause and practice mindful perception (self-as-process), gently noticing "I see," "I hear," "I feel," as a way to reconnect with oneself or calm down from moments of high stress and narrowed perception.

- Clients can deepen their practice of self-as-context by broadening their awareness and asking themselves questions like:
  - "Who is noticing this?"
  - "I notice that I'm experiencing this—can I look at myself with kindness?"
  - "Can I become aware of my difficult experience—can I allow it to be here and keep up the confidence that the experience will change again?"
  - "Can I notice what I am experiencing and how stuck I feel? And can I broaden my perception to what else is there?"
- When clients ask themselves questions such as "Given this difficult experience—can I stay present, make space for it, and do what matters to me right now?" it can help them refocus on their values.

Encourage your clients to find their own words and integrate any parts of the exercises in this chapter into their daily routine, in whatever way feels helpful and sustainable for them. Together, you can look at these little practices in detail and evaluate them more often.

Evening reflections can promote relaxation, completion, and good sleep:

- Reviewing briefly what happened during the day
- Acknowledging what was difficult and what went well
- Appreciating even small moments of value or success

Structures are effective when they fit into the client's life, are easy to execute, and offer meaningful and motivating outcomes. Many years after they completed therapy, clients have told me that these practices helped them sustain progress, deepen their capacity for self-as-context, and live more in alignment with their values.

6.6 Conclusion

For clients to practice self-as-context effectively, several key layers need to be cultivated:

1. "I-Here-Now" as Direct Experience
   The foundation of self-as-context involves momentary perceptions, both within and outside of the body (self-as-process). These are simple, direct experiences: "I see this picture," "I feel my feet on the ground."
2. "I-Here-Now" Observing with Distance
   Clients can practice observing themselves or others (e.g. "I-there-now," "I-there-then," "you-there-now") with distance, from the vantage point of I-here-now ("I notice myself, sitting in the chair, feeling satisfied about the day," "I hear you, talking about this incident that happened earlier today"). This allows clients to witness events from different contexts or moments in time, which fosters detachment and deeper understanding (self-as-context—deictic perspective).
3. "I-Here-Now" Observing from a Hierarchical Perspective

Awareness expands into a broader perspective, incorporating purpose, compassion, and nonjudgmental observation ("I notice myself being excited about this possibility in the future," "I notice you feeling sad about this situation that happened last month"). Clients begin to integrate their experiences into a stable and encompassing view of the self, still noticing all of that from the perspective of I-here-now (self-as-context—hierarchical perspective).

Self-as-context experiences are abstract and require consistent practice, but with time, clients can access them more easily and sustain this perspective for longer. It's important to distinguish between self-as-context and automatic critical self-thoughts and memories. When critical thoughts or memories arise, clients can bring conscious awareness to them with questions like "Who is noticing these critical thoughts?"

When we practice these perspectives with clients, either (1) they can observe their experiences as if standing "behind the camera," watching events unfold, or (2) we can guide them to observe themselves as they engage in those experiences—stepping "in front of the camera," and seeing themselves through the lens of the observer. Both perspectives offer valuable insights. The application depends on your style and on the client's preferences.

6.7 Summary

This chapter compiles practical and impactful exercises addressing all three self-aspects:

- Practicing self-as-process
- Creating distance from self-as-content
- Engaging in perspective-taking to cultivate self-as-context

The approaches to developing self-as-context remain consistent across situations:

1. Building the foundation with your client by practicing self-as-process, which means recognizing and naming internal experiences. This can be done by adhering closely to direct perception, using phrases like "I feel..." or "I hear..."
2. Including perspective-taking by guiding clients to recognize that their perception is anchored in their "I," "here," and "now," and that multiple perspectives are possible. For example, "I-here-now" observing "I-there-now," or "I" remembering what "I-there-then" experienced, or "I" seeing "you-there-now."
3. Strengthening broader, hierarchical perspectives, incorporating elements such as self-compassion, compassion for others, nonjudgmental observation, or values as an orientation for actions. Recognizing more clearly that "I" and "you" are not only separate but also connected; for example, "I" may feel what "you-there-then" felt, or "we" together looking into the same direction. The hierarchical perspective also entails integrating all parts of the self, understanding that one is more than any experience. For instance, "I notice this difficult thought, I can create distance from it, and I can see that this thought is part of myself, but I am bigger than this thought."

Allowing and exploring self-as-context experiences can be life-changing and sometimes beyond words.

All exercises can be adapted to a client's situation and context. The key is maintaining awareness of your therapeutic intention—identifying which process you aim to practice—and staying flexible in response to the client's intentions and reactions.

We explored questions designed to strengthen self-as-process and self-as-context, while also identifying the potential short-term benefits of hindering self-as-content. You are now equipped to recognize progress in all three self-aspects.

Finally, we discussed how to establish manageable and rewarding structures to support clients in maintaining their new behaviors over time.

> Self-as-context helped me a lot during a time of intense physical and emotional pain. It allowed me to create more space for myself. The observing part enabled me to step back and separate from my thoughts and feelings. I could witness them without condemning myself. It was a period of pain, sadness, and loss—and I acknowledged that pain, offering myself love and self-compassion, trusting that it would eventually pass.
>
> —Hannah, forty-eight years old, social worker

CHAPTER 7

The Therapeutic Relationship: Your Most Important Tool

As therapists, we rely on one overarching tool that is always present in our work: the therapeutic relationship. It serves as the foundation for successful collaboration, aligning our efforts with the client's goals and values. We could say that we are other-as-context for our clients.

But how do we cultivate a strong, effective relationship? What enables us to truly connect and build trust?

Research suggests that the same processes of change consistently identified in therapy studies (Hofmann et al., 2021) are also integral to fostering a meaningful therapeutic relationship. However, it's not enough to simply discuss these processes in theory; what truly matters is how we embody them in practice. When therapists demonstrate flexibility, genuine interest, respect, and compassion, the outcomes of therapy improve significantly (Walser, Karlin, Trockel, Mazina, & Taylor, 2013; Svitak, 2021).

7.1 Metaphor for Being Other-as-Context

Like all of us, I cultivate the therapeutic relationship from the first "Welcome to my practice" to the moment when the client and I celebrate their progress and acknowledge that they no longer need my support.

I carry an internal image of the therapeutic relationship and in some cases I make it explicit through a physical metaphor—for instance, when clients struggle to build trust or when we explore particularly unsettling topics. I often use this approach when I believe a conscious, safe connection is essential.

There are different ways to introduce this metaphor. I might begin by asking my client if they can get aware of the outer boundaries of their body—a concept they typically grasp easily. Then I invite them to notice the invisible space around them—the area they might consider "theirs," or their personal space. Most of them understand straightaway, but if not, I briefly lean my head very close to theirs. The immediate discomfort usually clarifies what I mean, as it feels like an intrusion. Typically, clients describe this invisible space as extending about an arm's length around them. I don't know exactly how they visualize it, but for me, it feels more like a cloud than a room with fixed walls.

I then point out that I also sit here with my body and my own personal space. As a therapist, I offer to expand my space toward them, creating a shared room into which they can expand. I ask them how they experience this shared room and the feedback is usually positive—mostly something like "it feels open," or "inviting," or "comforting." No one has ever responded with "I don't know what you are talking about," but if that were to happen, I wouldn't insist. Not every metaphor works for everyone, and I might instead explore their perspective on our relationship.

Once we have established this physical metaphor, we can explore what unfolds in the shared space emerging from our relationship. When difficult topics arise, I might ask, "Are you willing to share this with me by imagining placing it into our shared space and letting it be there for a while so we can observe what happens?"

I consider this practice an embodied version of self-as-context, offering several therapeutic benefits:

- Ownership and agency: Clients actively choose to share or not share their difficult content, often leading to new perspectives and awareness of further meaningful actions.
- Distance and perspective: By viewing their challenges as objects within the shared space, clients gain distance and a more hierarchical perspective, recognizing that they are more than their struggles.
- Collaborative exploration: The shared space fosters collaboration, allowing therapist and client to jointly consider the best course of action.

As therapists, we serve as other-as-context for our clients. When our perspective on them is non-judgmental, clear, and accepting, they may feel free to express themselves, and something begins to shift. This neutral, grounded perspective also helps us, as therapists, to find more valuable responses.

This inviting context is especially important for clients who have experienced neglect or a lack of connection in childhood or adulthood. The hopeful message is that they can still learn to develop missing capacities, for example noticing and naming internal experiences. By practicing within a safe, shared space, they can begin to develop their own self-as-context, integrate and accept their experiences, trust themselves and others, and create a more flexible-yet-stable sense of self.

7.2 Our Listening

One client who did that exercise with me took a significant step toward acknowledging her sadness about repeatedly entering harmful relationships. She had believed she needed a man to feel emotionally cared for. For the first time, she entertained the idea that she could care for herself—a concept that felt foreign to her. When I asked what allowed her to take this new perspective, she paused thoughtfully and finally said, "I think today I listened to myself for the first time."

This is what we offer our clients through the space we create: our listening, which allows them to listen to themselves more deeply. When we embody "I am here and open to listen to you," we provide that space. Painful experiences mostly need to be shared and heard at some point. Sharing and being met with openness leads to acceptance and getting unstuck, which allows new movement and growth. Open listening acts like a magnet—anything can arise. This creates a salutary space for clients, who are sometimes surprised by what emerges within themselves.

Not every client feels safe to step into the space we provide. For many, starting therapy can feel daunting. For clients holding onto a maladaptive self-concept, it may even feel life-threatening. While they desire self-expansion, it often requires relinquishing a self-concept that, despite being limiting, has provided stability and orientation in adverse life circumstances. This tension makes the process of learning slow, often progressing in tiny, incremental steps. As therapists, accompanying this journey can be deeply rewarding, but also exhausting and, at times, even frustrating. We may feel as though nothing we provide is sufficient or quite "the right thing."

In these moments, we might consider expanding our own space.

7.3 Expanding Your Space

Each therapist is a unique individual, and we each have our own body, genetics, personality, abilities, experiences, culture, knowledge, current state, willingness, and more. We can offer perspective and space both to ourselves (self-as-context) and to others (other-as-context).

Everyone perceives their clients differently, asks different questions, and possesses a unique mix of flexibility in the processes we use in our work. Using the physical metaphor, we could say, "The space we provide for our clients is unique to each of us." If our clients choose to continue working with us after the initial session, we can infer that their experience felt aligned with their goals and values. In other words, we could say that the space we create resonates with them and feels like the right fit.

An open and accepting space encourages clients to share things they may not have felt comfortable sharing before. There are several ways for practicing being open and intentional as a therapist:

- Verbally expressing interest by saying something like, "I'm really curious about this experience you mentioned more frequently—it seems to be important to you," can encourage clients to develop greater curiosity and interest in themselves.
- Approaching the session consciously with an internal stance of openness and curiosity.
- Working with our own internal experiences, integrating difficult content as it arises in our lives.
- Modeling acceptance and self-awareness in session with our own content when appropriate.

As therapists, we can work with difficult content in our own lives by approaching our painful experiences with curiosity and openness, giving them space through our breath, and accepting their presence. When we face our own vulnerability and perceived flaws without shying away, we gain credibility as therapists in encouraging our clients to confront their own dark corners. We have more compassion for them because we know how much courage it takes to engage with the challenging sides of the self, to integrate them, and to discover new facets of personal growth.

I've often found that the new perspectives I've gained on a difficult topic have become valuable resources in my work with clients.

7.4 My Journey to Expand My Self

In the following paragraphs, I will share part of my own journey, highlighting the flexibility processes that were either lacking or particularly helpful. While your life circumstances may differ from mine, I believe that if you embark on a search, you will discover your own unique way to integrate these processes into your life.

During a meditation seminar, the instructor invited us participants to say "good morning" to the most important person in our lives. My immediate thought was, "Oh, my husband isn't here," until I realized the instructor was referring to me.

I had been so focused on caring for others that I never saw self-care as a priority (getting present, gaining perspective on myself). One of my favorite sayings at that time was "I can sleep in my grave when I'm dead," meaning it didn't matter if I slept only four or five hours a night for years.

Eventually, this mindset led me into severe exhaustion. Over time, I developed chronic pain in various parts of my body and struggled with terrible sleep disturbances. The most alarming impact for me, however, was the fatigue I felt during therapy sessions. I would become so drained that I could feel myself fading. Clients even asked kindly if I'd like to take a nap before continuing our session, or stated, "You seem to be really tired today."

This was not who I wanted to be as a therapist (self-as-context, values, commitment). I felt devastated (presence). It became clear that if I didn't make a radical shift (acceptance, commitment), I would no longer be able to help anyone. This tough realization forced me to confront how much I had neglected my own well-being while trying to prioritize others (self-as-context, values, commitment). While some of my overcommitment stemmed from genuine external demands, there was also a deep belief that I had to constantly provide and care for others to feel worthy (self-as-content). When I became physically unwell and felt "useless," I didn't particularly like myself (presence, self-as-context).

Accepting my physical limits—and the accompanying feelings of failure and insufficiency—wasn't easy (acceptance). In my mind, this was a catastrophe. I worried endlessly: If I didn't stay up late working on my projects, who would take them on? Everyone else was already overwhelmed. And what about the hundreds of unread emails? Would people feel disappointed or neglected (fusion)?

But my body forced me to take my own well-being seriously, and I did the necessary steps (commitment). I began visiting doctors and following their advice. I created boundaries, such as shutting down my computer at 8 p.m. and going to bed by 10 p.m. I started scheduling my days realistically and accepting that I couldn't fit everything in (acceptance). I let go of certain responsibilities and allowed myself to feel the difficult emotions that arose (presence, acceptance). I took time for leisure, resting on the sofa, cooking healthy meals, and going for walks (commitment). Gradually, my sleep improved, my energy returned, and I found a much better balance.

Some of my fears did come true—some people were disappointed, and initially, parts of my projects seemed to get stuck. In the end, though, solutions were found for everything, and nothing collapsed. Interestingly, stepping back from some of my projects created space for others to step in, leading to greater long-term growth, which continues to this day.

The most challenging step for me as a therapist was being open about my sleep disturbances with my clients. I never knew if I would suddenly feel fatigued during a session. This uncertainty led to significant tension and effort on my part, which resulted in even more exhaustion. So, I decided to address it openly, even though it felt shameful and vulnerable, and I was concerned about how clients might perceive it.

During the initial consultation, I shared that I suffer from sleep issues and that I never know when fatigue might set in. I told the client that I would mention it if I noticed it happening and that they were also welcome to bring it up. I offered to end the session if they felt it was no longer effective due to my fatigue, assuring them that there would be no costs in that case.

I was surprised by the understanding responses from my clients, and I only once had to end a session due to fatigue. Remembering these experiences and how hard it was for me to take those steps often helps me in my everyday work as a therapist.

Maybe this inspires you to look at your own self-expansion, which not only benefits you, but also creates more space for your clients, giving them the room to grow and thrive.

7.5 Providing a Transformational Context in Session

Here are several practices I have found useful in preparing myself for work with my clients. They are tailored to my personal preferences and to my context of working in private practice with fifty-minute sessions. I hope they can help you uncover the structures that best suit your own context.

7.5.1 Preparing Myself

Before heading to work, I like to sit on a meditation cushion for a few minutes and take some mindful breaths to connect with myself. When I'm running late, I do it on my bicycle. I focus first on making sure that I feel safe and well cared for, and then on the intention that my work today will serve my clients and support their growth. I reflect on whether there's anything particularly important to me for the day. If anything unresolved arises, I make an agreement with myself about when I'll address it and then set it aside. This practice helps me create a supportive context for myself and remain grounded and focused.

At the office, before a session, I briefly review the content of the last session. I connect internally first with myself, and then with my client, by reflecting on our agreed intention for the overall therapy goals. I adopt an open, neutral stance, ready to listen curiously to how things have been for them and what new issues might arise. With this preparation, I'm ready to be fully present, making my client the most important person in the room during their session, while also staying in touch with my own internal feedback.

7.5.2 Starting Therapy

In the first session, I share with a new client what's important to me:

- Active collaboration: "We will do more than just talk. I often use exercises to make new steps experiential for you. When you have tried out something new in session already, it is much easier for you to repeat it in your daily life outside the therapy room."
- Feedback: "I will need your honest feedback on how what I offer works for you. While I'm the expert in my therapeutic method, you're the expert in your life. Bringing both together mostly leads to something meaningful and effective for clients."
- Client-led direction: "You set the direction based on what matters most to you. If that's unclear right now, we'll work together to figure it out. You have my full commitment to supporting your goals and values, but successful therapy will also require your full engagement."
- Transparency: "I'm transparent with no hidden agenda. You're welcome to ask at any time about my intentions, why I ask certain questions, or why I suggest a specific exercise."

- A safe relationship: "We'll develop a genuine relationship as two human beings, even though it will take place within a therapeutic framework and focus only on your needs. Everything that's important to you is welcome to show up in our relationship. Together, we'll look at it, and you can safely try new things."
- Flexibility: "After this first session, you can decide if you would like to continue or not, and either choice is fine—there's no need to justify your decision. Likewise, I would let you know if I think I'm not the right therapist to support you."
- Ending therapy: "When you decide to work with me, you can end therapy whenever you choose. My only request is that we find a good conclusion together. If you want to stop during a challenging phase of therapy, I might suggest continuing for a little longer, but ultimately, the decision is yours."

Once clients return their intake questionnaires, I conduct an assessment and create a treatment plan based on a network analysis (see chapter 5). I share this plan with them to ensure they feel seen and aligned with the approach. Clients are then encouraged to provide input if something seems misunderstood or if they have a different perspective.

7.5.3 Ongoing Therapy

Clients also receive a session feedback form (adapted from Tsai et al., 2009), which has two parts:

1. To be completed shortly after the session:
    - How did you experience our session? Thoughts, feelings, insights?
    - How helpful was the session (on a scale of 0–10)?
    - What was helpful or not helpful?
    - What could have made the session more helpful or a better experience? Is there anything that is difficult for you to say or ask for?
    - How connected did you feel to your therapist (on a scale of 0–10)?
    - How engaged were you during the session (on a scale of 0–10)?
    - What issues came up in the session/with your therapist that are similar to problems in your daily life?
    - What risks did you take in the session/with your therapist, or what progress did you make toward your values?
    - Did you do anything to move away from your values?
    - What from this session could translate into your life, and what would you like to practice or try after the session?

This part helps clients reflect on their internal experiences, progress, and engagement, ensuring the session's content isn't lost in daily life. I review their feedback either before or in the next session to ground the therapy in their immediate experiences, rather than my assumptions.

Some essential turning points have come from clients' honest answers to questions like "What was not helpful?" and "On a scale of one to ten, how connected did you feel to your therapist?" So long as we are open to listening, when we invite honest feedback, it encourages clients to engage more actively and take responsibility for their process—often leading to progress in therapy.

2. To be completed shortly before the next session:

- What have you done since the last session that was in line with your values? What was the impact?
- What have you done since the last session that was against your values? What was the impact? Was it important for something?
- What are your topics and concerns for today's session?
- How open have you been in responding to the questions (on a scale of 0–100)?
- Is there anything you'd like to add?

This section helps clients distinguish between value-consistent and value-inconsistent behavior, and explore the functionality of their actions ("It was important to me not to upset my mother, so I said yes even though I didn't want to."). By filling out this form, clients actively shape the therapy process as informed partners.

Most clients find the questionnaire helpful. For those who dislike it, I explore what makes it difficult. I don't insist they use it but incorporate some of the questions into our sessions instead.

7.5.4 Within Session

When you practice and internalize flexibility processes in your own life, they naturally become available for you, and you can weave them into your dialogue in session. You can engage in fluid conversations while continuously observing: Is the client open or avoiding? Are they present or caught up in racing thoughts? Are they self-aware or stuck in blaming mode? Are they moving toward their values or repeating unproductive patterns?

For clients with rigid self-concepts, it's crucial to step back from your own assumptions and reflect from time to time: "What might be preventing this client from taking a new perspective? How can I create space for new facets of their identity to emerge? What might I have missed hearing so far?" You cannot know the answers in advance; you can only listen.

7.6 Conclusion

The therapeutic space we create serves as a constant contextual factor that we offer to our clients. The space invites them to engage, and in doing so, they bring their own space into the dynamic. This mutual interplay relies on the capacity, willingness, and practice of both therapist and client.

When nurtured, this shared space becomes a foundation for growth, connection, and meaningful change. This is the magic of therapy: insights lead to shifts, new behaviors occur that once seemed unimaginable, and new, fulfilling facets of the client's identity naturally unfold.

The principles are simple, yet often difficult to apply: it's about learning to observe inner and outer experiences, and adopting different perspectives—for both the therapist and the client. We can cultivate these capacities ourselves, and—with suitable interventions—make them accessible to our clients. Strengthening these skills can lead to a new level of awareness and understanding that may last for a lifetime. One client described it this way: "I've carried this pain with me for decades. But after today's session, it feels neutral. It doesn't weigh on me anymore."

7.7 Summary

Our most important tool as therapists, present in every session, is the therapeutic relationship. We can refer to it as "other-as-context" or "the space we provide"—self-as-context personalized in the presence of another person. This physical metaphor helps both clients and therapists connect more consciously, recognize barriers in the relationship, and explore new, enriching perspectives.

As therapists, we can:

- Verbally express our interest in the client's difficult content during sessions, showing openness and care.
- Communicate through presence by adopting an open, curious stance, even without verbalizing it explicitly.
- Work with our own internal experiences, integrating difficult content as it arises in our life.
- Model acceptance and self-awareness in session with our own content when appropriate.

You've also been provided with examples of how to cultivate a transformational context by preparing for sessions in meaningful ways. Hopefully, these examples will inspire you to develop your own effective structures.

> The process of opening up to a therapeutic relationship in which I was seen with kindness allowed me to expand my own sense of self in relation to others. At first, experiencing a shared space shaped by trust, responsibility, and a mature understanding felt unsettling. But as I accepted these feelings, it enabled me to grow and take more agency in shaping my life and actions.
>
> The sessions did not magically solve everything, but they gave me the opportunity to cultivate an attitude toward myself, the world, and others that aligns with my own values. This made it easier to act with purpose in the beautiful mess we call life. I am deeply grateful for that.
>
> —Anne, thirty-seven years old, clinician

CHAPTER 8

Self-as-Context Applied in Real Life

Self-as-context is a social capacity that strengthens our relationships—both with ourselves and others. It helps us cultivate compassion, adopt diverse perspectives, and become more aware of values-based actions.

The ability to recognize, respect, exchange and align different viewpoints is essential for effective problem-solving, whether it's on an individual level, within groups, or on a global scale.

In the following sections, I present some examples of how self-as-context can be applied in different areas of life—whether for personal growth, for couples, in small or large groups, across different cultures, or helping clients facing death.

8.1 Self-Love

Love is not merely a feeling, though it can feel wonderful. More than that, love is a stance—a deliberate and at times demanding practice that requires us to step beyond what feels easy or comfortable in the moment. For example, caring for a sick child in the middle of the night, when all you want is to sleep, doesn't feel romantic or fulfilling. And yet, we still do it as an act of love. But while it can be comparatively easy to care for others, it's often harder to practice love for ourselves—or, in other words, to practice self-as-context.

8.1.1 How to Love Yourself

Loving yourself doesn't require liking yourself. You don't have to like your body, your thoughts, your feelings, or even your current situation. Your aversions shape you as much as your preferences—sometimes even more. Self-love is about embracing all of it—noticing your experiences with curiosity and placing them in the context of what truly matters to you, bringing fulfillment in the long term.

Self-as-context offers a framework for self-love. It allows you to create space for your experiences and bring love to them in practical ways. You don't need to transform your experiences into something different or extraordinary—this is you, and you are more than all of your experiences. Through this lens, self-love becomes an honest practice of self-awareness and alignment with your heart's desires.

I often encourage clients to shift from "must mode" to "lust mode," exploring what genuinely brings them joy. So, what do you really want to integrate into your life? What are you "hungry for"?

8.1.2 Daily Acts of Love

At its core, love is an everyday action. Show yourself that you are loved by at least one person: yourself. You can give yourself small moments to look forward to and enjoy, such as:

- Cuddling in bed for a few extra minutes
- Stretching your precious body
- Drinking your favorite tea or coffee
- Cooking something nurturing
- Sharing a loving embrace with your child
- Taking a walk with your dog, smelling the fresh air
- Calling a friend

The key is to engage in these moments with awareness and remind yourself, "I treasure this experience; it nourishes me." Otherwise, the mind defaults to autopilot, and you miss the moment.

As one client put it, "When I did good things for myself, I kept waiting for the good feelings to come, but they never did." The game changer came when she discovered the power of her stance: consciously approaching an action with the mindset, "I do this because I value myself."

8.1.3 Creating a Supportive Structure

A well-crafted structure is like a safety net, catching us before we fall. Ideally, it feels like a hammock, providing space to relax and recharge before we serve others again. When looking at your weekly schedule, ask yourself if you see moments that feel like a hammock. Take this seriously, as the better you become at cultivating a nurturing lifestyle for yourself, the more creative and resourceful you can be with your clients.

Even mini-breaks throughout the day—taking two or three conscious breaths at your desk, in the bathroom, or on the way to the coffee machine—can help you reconnect with yourself. You might ask yourself, "Everything okay? Do you need anything?" Or, when you find yourself ruminating, you might guide your focus with a beneficial image—like your favorite place in nature—or a supportive sentence to encourage yourself.

As therapists who offer unconditional acceptance to our clients every day, we need a handful of people with whom we can have fun and feel safe expressing whatever is present for us. What kinds of connection feel most nourishing to you?

We spend our days serving others, so moments of solitude—where no one needs anything from us—can be incredibly restorative. Scheduling leisure time for a hike, a swim, or simply being lazy is a powerful way to ensure you honor those moments.

Finally, if spirituality is part of your life, connecting to a greater power can provide a sense of being held—especially during challenging times. When you don't feel capable of loving yourself, perhaps you can leave it to this greater power and wrap yourself in its love. When feelings or responsibilities are too overwhelming to bear alone, a broader perspective can help carry them. Asking for blessings or guidance can support you in aligning your actions with your deeper values. You can integrate this practice into your preparation for therapy sessions, intending that your work nurtures your clients' growth and well-being.

8.2 Self-as-Context for Couples

We often believe that love depends on finding the "right" person—someone who embodies the qualities we admire. We think, "You're so beautiful, so smart, so funny, so charming—I love you." But this mindset can trap us, because if those qualities fade or change, we might feel our love fading, too.

What if, instead, we felt attracted to someone because they awakened our own capacity to love? Because they make it easier for us to practice love—perhaps by making us feel at home, able to be natural, without pretense, and to fulfill important life directions and yearnings? Because they reveal new facets of ourselves, helping us expand our ability to give space, to accept, and to create a welcoming context for both our own experiences and theirs?

A relationship becomes interesting when the other person doesn't behave as we'd like, when love no longer feels easy or pleasant, when the person does't look so beautiful, says things we disagree with, or becomes less funny. That's where the real practice begins. Who do we want to be then? How do we want to behave? Love as a feeling ebbs and flows, but love as a stance can endure, as long as we're willing to embody it.

I was lucky to learn this through my husband—he is a master of unconditional love. From the moment he decided I was the woman of his life, he never wavered. At first, I found it irritating. How could he be so persistent with his love, with me, an unlovable person? I thought it was a sign of weakness, and I challenged him by being emotional and unkind, especially when he didn't do what I expected.

We struggled a lot in those early years. But we were both committed to seeking support and growth opportunities. Humor helped as well, and more than thirty years later, when we're working together in the kitchen, I can say, "Oh my god, how can one person manage to do so many things wrong in such a short time!" and he'll reply with his irresistible smile, "That's because I have a special talent for doing things wrong."

Love doesn't always feel good. Yet, when we act with love, the feeling may return over time.

8.2.1 Breaking Cycles of Hurt and Blame

When things don't go well, love often unfolds differently. Many of us have been caught in exchanges like:

- "You're so distant."
- "That's because you yelled at me."
- "I yelled because you stopped talking to me."
- "You hurt me—it's your fault."

These conversations often feel like endless loops. Blame fuels anger, helplessness, and vulnerability, leaving us dependent on the other person's behavior to feel okay again.

A different perspective is to acknowledge that hurt is a natural part of close relationships. The closer someone is to us, the more likely they are to touch our sensitive spots. In couples therapy, I call this a "provision of service." Partners (and children) seem uniquely skilled at highlighting our sore points, offering us the chance to bring awareness and care to them. This perspective often helps interrupt destructive patterns and supports us in taking the next step.

8.2.2 Taking Responsibility for One's Own Pain

When we recognize that taking care of our pain is our own responsibility—not someone else's—we can practice self-as-context. It means allowing ourselves to feel hurt without becoming consumed by self-pity. It allows us to first respond with compassion for ourselves, starting with taking the time to comfort our wounded selves. This helps us calm our emotions and consider our next steps intentionally—for example, sharing with a trusted person, asking our partner for a conversation, or setting clear boundaries if necessary.

If someone intentionally and persistently harms us, we may need additional support to navigate the situation and find distance from that person.

8.2.3 Love as a Practice of Values and Growth

Love, like any capacity, can be developed throughout our lives. It becomes easier when we align with our values. I often ask my clients, "How do you want to act, even when the other person behaves in ways you dislike or even find terrible? How will you see this moment thirty years from now?"

Or how would you look back on torturing your partner with statements like:

- "You cannot fall asleep now, even if it's midnight—we need to talk this out."
- "How can you do this to me? You know how devastating it is for me."
- "You have always been like this—I knew you were a loser."

Self-as-context helps us refrain from saying those sentences when they come to mind, allowing us instead to stay silent and attend to what needs care within ourselves. We might call this authenticity—a life grounded in what truly matters to us. In my experience, the long-term reward is inner peace and freedom.

8.2.4 Love Is a Risk

Love in all its forms—whether friendship, family, pets, or romantic connection—is inherently risky. It opens us to disappointment, pain, and the possibility of losing someone through separation or death. Yet the alternative—a life without love—is even more disheartening and, as research shows, detrimental to our well-being.

David Schnarch (2011) suggests that intimate relationships are a perfect field for personal growth. He argues that our frustrations in these relationships have contributed significantly to human development. To sustain a long-term, loving relationship, we must endure tension and fear, developing autonomy alongside connection. This process is rarely easy, often accompanied by conflict, but it cultivates resilience, adaptability, and inner strength.

This perspective aligns with the ACT approach: suffering is not an error or an accident, but an integral part of life and personal growth. The goal is not to avoid suffering but to avoid adding suffering through unhelpful patterns of avoidance or clinging.

8.2.5 Building Deep, Fulfilling Relationships

John and Julie Gottman (2024) emphasize the importance of positive interactions in maintaining long-term relationships. Their research shows that a 5:1 ratio of positive to negative interactions during conflicts—and a 20:1 ratio in daily life—is necessary for a fulfilling relationship. This can feel challenging, but it's worth striving for.

One exercise I recommend for couples or any long-term relationship is this: at the end of each day, take a moment to recognize each other. One partner begins by sharing three things they appreciate about themselves, followed by three things they appreciate about the other. Then, it's the other partner's turn.

With practice, this exercise becomes richer and more natural:

- "I appreciate that you helped me solve this problem today."
- "I admire how you went to work despite not feeling like it."
- "I'm grateful you stayed calm when our daughter provoked you."
- "Thanks for visiting your dad."

This small ritual strengthens connection and reinforces a sense of mutual appreciation.

When we commit to a long-term relationship, we practice trust and openness. This cannot remain a mental exercise; it requires courageous action. We extend confidence, lower our defenses, and share our inner worlds.

After taking a bold step, self-as-context offers the space to reflect: What worked? What didn't? What might be missing—on our side, theirs, or both? From this reflection, we can decide what to adjust, what to request, and how to create safer and deeper connections.

This is the pathway I see to developing long-term, deeply fulfilling relationships. It's not without challenges, but the growth, strength, and love it fosters make it profoundly worthwhile.

8.3 Self-as-Context in Groups

Every person belongs to various social networks: friendship circles, family, colleagues, sports teams, NGOs, neighbors, book clubs, parents' groups, communities, neighborhoods, congregations, and platforms like TikTok, Instagram, and Facebook, as well as groups on email or Zoom, to name just a few.

Through psychotherapy, we influence how our clients function and interact within their social networks. Helping clients find and cultivate well-disposed networks can turn these relationships into stabilizing factors for their mental health. Groups can either support or undermine their goals—for instance, sticking to a sugar-free diet is easier within a health-conscious friend group but far more challenging among fast food enthusiasts.

Therapy becomes more impactful when clients anchor new behaviors within their networks. Here are a few examples from my practice:

- A teacher struggling with students with behavioral problems stopped trying to be the nice guy and instead set clearer rules. As a result, they reported better classroom management and more effective lessons; this, in turn, fostered respect and collaboration among their students.
- A school administrator used therapy-inspired insights to organize a workshop for principals, encouraging values-driven leadership and teamwork.
- Another client developed determination and rallied family members to coordinate care for their aging parents.
- A single mom established a co-parenting arrangement with two fathers for her child, earning the respect of extended family members for this unconventional-yet-effective solution.
- A client experiencing burnout realized that his work environment encouraged overworking, provided minimal support, and was at times even hostile. He decided to leave and find a new job.

These shifts may seem simple, but they rarely are. They are always transformational for the individual, and sometimes for their environment as well. Occasionally, growth requires leaving workplaces or people behind.

8.3.1 Empathy Becomes a Challenge

More and more often, I meet clients who are deeply affected by the global situation. They struggle to cope with the constant stream of media reports about deteriorating economies, autocratic political structures, violence, displacement, starvation, and natural disasters with devastating consequences.

Even though most of these events involve people they don't personally know, they still feel the impact. As social beings, our evolutionary advantage lies in cooperation, which is deeply tied to empathy. It's in our nature to recognize and respond to the emotions of others.

For millennia, empathy was confined to small, manageable tribes or communities. But cultural evolution and technological advancements have dramatically expanded our horizons. Our genetic, biological, and psychological makeup can't keep up and our capacity for empathy is often stretched to its limits (Hayes, 2015).

However, nature also built in a "safety mechanism"—our ability to categorize others as different or "other." This mechanism allows us to reduce empathy, devaluing or dehumanizing others, blaming them, and rejecting their views. We can disconnect internally. And as humans with language, we can rationalize and even justify intentional harm, believing we are acting rightly. We can prioritize our own interests over the well-being or even the lives of others.

This behavior is clearly visible on social media and contributes to a growing sense of helplessness for many. In the long run, this kind of disconnection rarely serves the greater good. It benefits only a minority and fails to resolve global problems, or it might even worsen them.

While empathy is an innate part of our evolutionary makeup, compassion is not. Compassion—and self-compassion—are conscious capacities that must be learned and cultivated through social interaction. Taking another person's perspective means connecting with them and attempting to feel what they feel. It becomes significantly harder to harm others when we are aware of the pain we cause.

8.3.2 How Can We Empower Clients?

For clients who feel overwhelmed by humanity's seemingly unsolvable challenges, at first, resignation ("I cannot do much anyway"), reducing empathy ("I cannot deal with that, I have my own problems"), or neglecting their own well-being ("First thing in the morning and last thing at night, I check different news channels") may seem like solutions.

As therapists, we can acknowledge our clients who care about the world. We can ask them about the feelings that come up when they face those challenges and disasters. Practicing self-as-context can help them start with self-compassion—allowing space for their helplessness, sadness, fear, or anger, feeling it, and accepting it (Hayes, 2015). There is much in the world to feel anger and sorrow about, but there is also much to be done.

A next step can be finding actionable ways to cope with feelings of overwhelm. These might include committed actions, such as donating to disaster relief; demonstrating for an important cause; sending love, light, and prayers; or temporarily stepping back from news consumption to prioritize their own well-being.

Some clients choose to focus on themselves, their families, or their friends, fostering a more loving world within their immediate reach. One client who was deeply distressed about an ongoing war realized that she wanted to resolve her own personal "war," a long-standing conflict with a colleague.

Others find empowerment through political engagement, volunteering with NGOs, or contributing in their own ways, like offering soccer training for kids. Still others engage in meaningful discussions with friends or people with contrary views, using conversation as a tool for connection and change.

The path a client may choose depends on their energy levels and life circumstances. It should be valuable for them, sustainable in the long run, and enhance their sense of self-efficacy.

It is important for all of us to stay functional. Practicing self-as-context and compassion does not mean losing ourselves in the suffering of others or taking it on as our own. Rather, it means staying connected with ourselves while expanding our awareness toward other people.

The vantage point of our awareness carries no emotions itself—it is sober or neutral, yet still connected and compassionate. We are not at the mercy of our empathy.

This inner flexibility can serve as a foundation for deepening our openness and compassion, helping us navigate the complexity of our modern, globally interconnected world with clarity and care.

Being able to say, "The world isn't how I would create it, but I do what I can within my reach," marks a profound shift. If more people cultivated self-as-context in this way, we might become more creative and discover better solutions to both local and global challenges together.

How do we embrace a global context? As a species, we don't fully know yet—we're still learning.

8.3.3 The Role of Therapy in Societal Change

When clients are stepping out of their narrow, often painful personal perspective, they gain a better understanding of how they function and contribute within a larger context—whether in their family, work teams, sports clubs, political groups, or music groups. They expand their perspective on themselves. Acknowledging their broader potential can enable them to transform patterns of suffering into meaningful and productive action.

Since becoming a therapist, I have understood psychotherapeutic processes and training methods as tools for building societies that are more humane, vibrant, and healthy. In such societies, the need for therapy might diminish—especially if we introduce our powerful tools to young people, as is already happening in many places.

8.4 Self-as-Context in Diverse Cultures

I have worked with people around the world, and there is a remarkable alignment regarding shared goals and values. People desire health and peace for themselves and their communities, sufficient food, education for their children, and a promising future. Most of them are willing to work toward these goals, as it brings them meaning and dignity—crucial elements of a fulfilling life (Hayes, 2019).

In Sierra Leone, West Africa, I led numerous workshops for healthcare workers and other professionals, many of whom had endured or witnessed the horrors of a decade-long civil war. They had lost loved ones or suffered lasting physical and mental harm; some, as former child soldiers, had been forced to commit acts of violence.

People in Sierra Leone are often deeply religious (peacefully within the religions, mostly Muslim and Christian), and a common coping strategy was to seek explanations, questioning what they might have done to anger God and bring such punishment upon themselves. Some former child soldiers, even fifteen years later, were not allowed to return to their villages or families because the community wanted nothing to do with "murderers."

Acceptance exercises and bigger perspectives provided participants with noticeable relief. They no longer needed explanations, but instead allowed themselves to feel their pain and integrate it as part of their self. Through values identification, it became clear how often meaningful things had emerged from suffering. A former child soldier, for instance, now worked in social services with street boys involved in gang-related robberies. He immediately applied the learned ACT exercises in his work. Another social worker who lost a big part of his vision in an attack and could no longer become a priest had dedicated himself to helping those with visual impairments. He realized that he was living the same values he would have embodied as a priest and finally found peace with his life's undesired turn.

Former soldiers who had become motorbike taxi drivers, notorious for aggression and rule breaking, formed an association after a workshop. They established shared values and rules, and took pride in upholding them. Years later, I met them again. Though little had changed in terms of poverty, they had managed to build a clubhouse where they gathered to sustain their values-based community.

All of the described moves required shifts in perspective and enhancement of the self.

Self-as-context was a significant component in all workshops. After building some confidence within the group, a frequent exercise was "Eyes On," where participants sit knee-to-knee, looking into each other's eyes without speaking. This contradicts cultural norms that discourage close proximity and eye contact, especially between men and women, young people and adults, or in hierarchical relationships. However, participants trusted us trainers, and they were moved by the experience of seeing the humanity in each other, regardless of gender, skin color, or rank. A strong sense of connection arose, and people opened up, sharing their stories.

All participants worked with people in some capacity—they were therapists, teachers, police officers, spiritual leaders, chiefs, and others. In subsequent supervision sessions and workshops, we often heard that they were now able to help their people more effectively. We heard moving stories from their work with ACT: street boys willing to surrender their knives after an exercise; a former child soldier asking a relative to mediate his reintegration into his village community; a social worker, severely injured during the war, standing up to help abused girls.

Local social workers began leading their own workshops and established a local NGO that continues to grow to this day. Over the years, they have worked with hundreds of communities and thousands of people, applying the learned therapeutic tools to transform their culture from the inside out.

Community leaders now turn to them for support in implementing projects aimed at reducing gender-based violence, increasing food security for starving families, and providing education as an alternative to early marriage for girls.

Our own actions and those of our clients can impact communities on many levels, even globally. This is only possible when we transcend our self-image and adopt new perspectives—prioritizing our shared humanity and values over differences and discomfort.

To deal with our global challenges, we will need to step outside of our comfort zones. We need to extend trust in the face of cultural gaps and recognize our discomfort, as well as the fact that we think we "know better." By practicing the observer perspective, we naturally bring others into our view. We intuitively know that, in the long run, a good life is something we can only achieve together as humanity. Let's dare to dream—for ourselves and our clients—far beyond symptom reduction.

What do we gain from this? Each person discovers the answer to that individually. It's an invitation to think outside the box. Every day, we have countless opportunities to plant seeds for a better future, even if we may not live to see it.

8.5 Self-as-Context for Dealing with the Dying

My last point in this book is the one certainty we all share in life: that we will die. During my time working in an elderly home and in hospice care, I accompanied people passing away. I found it rewarding. It's natural and happens to everyone. Yet, we struggle to fully imagine it happening to us—just as we can't envision being old when we're young.

As therapists, we encounter clients facing death in different forms:

- Coping with a terminal illness

- Grieving the loss of a loved one
- Experiencing fear of their own death
- Witnessing others die, whether naturally, through crime, or during natural disasters
- Dealing with the wish to die and suicidal thoughts

8.5.1 Offering a Larger Context

The essential point I want to emphasize is that our ability to provide a broader context when our clients are facing death is crucial to serving them effectively. The context we offer depends on our own learning history, our capacity to hold space, and our willingness to open ourselves to profound pain. To do so, we must also find a grounded and compassionate stance for ourselves.

For me, it is comforting to know: I am going to die. Any uncertainty about that would feel far more unsettling. Everything physical will eventually dissolve. This certainty gives me the freedom to live fully and choose a path that inspires me. I'm curious about new spaces and perspectives, and death seems like the final, fascinating experience of this life—both a mystery and a fact.

Losing loved ones to death, fearing their loss, and experiencing the suicide of a client have been some of my most painful encounters with death.

Being aware of that, I feel mostly unafraid to explore with clients what death means to them—what they fear, hope, regret, or grieve—while providing an open space for them to process these feelings. When appropriate, I am also willing to share from my own experiences.

I sometimes guide my clients to imagine themselves at an old age—maybe in a rocking chair on their veranda, knowing it will soon be time to let go—to picture how they ask themselves: Was this the life I wanted to live? Did I live it fully? Did I pursue what was important to me? How would it be to answer with a wholehearted "yes," and what would that mean for their life today? Are there any committed actions they would like to take now?

8.5.2 Supporting Those Left Behind

For those who remain, grieving the loss of a loved one can be excruciating and profoundly challenging to integrate. Self-as-context can be a vital tool for helping clients expand their inner space to hold their sadness, allowing it to be present—day by day, moment by moment, for as long as needed.

In different cultures, we refer to a "year of grief"—the first year after a loss, during which the mourner experiences all the seasons, holidays, and meaningful dates they once shared with the deceased. This process helps them gradually understand: I will live on, without this person. While the loved one remains a part of their life, it's in a different way. Over time, they learn to express and feel love and connectedness differently.

Though grief can be brutal, it's not static. Like all feelings, it evolves. Over time, the intensity often softens, fading into the background. That said, grief may return at any moment, in waves both large and small. Helping clients cultivate the willingness to sit with these emotions—even for a few minutes a day in the early months—can be profoundly beneficial.

I recall an eighty-year-old woman who came to me months after losing her healthy, eighty-four-year-old husband in a hiking accident. She told me their life had been "always good"—they had been kind with each other, raised four children and enjoyed their grandchildren—but now she felt stuck in her grief, unable to accept what had happened. She also struggled with self-critical thoughts like "I should be over this by now."

Having little prior experience with significant pain, she didn't know how to cope. Over two or three sessions, I guided her in using her breath to create space within her body for her feelings of pain and loss. With practice, she became more capable of handling her grief and eventually reached a place of acceptance and self-compassion. She was still sad, but not stuck any more.

Some losses are particularly difficult to accept, such as the death of a very young person or deaths that are unnatural or violent. Ultimately, our role is to create a space where pain and other feelings can be explored, felt, and integrated. This process helps clients move forward with the memories and love they carry, as they rebuild their lives in the absence of their loved one.

8.6 Conclusion

In this chapter, we explored how practicing self-as-context can be beneficial in various areas of life—whether in loving ourselves or others, collaborating within groups or across cultures, or coping with the experience of loss.

Self-as-context is not intended to be a one-size-fits-all solution, but rather a perspective we can adopt and cultivate in any situation. It offers a pathway to more flexible and creative responses, tailored to the specific challenges a person is facing.

The underlying practices for self-as-context remain consistent across all areas:

1. Build a strong foundation with your clients by practicing self-as-process with them. This involves recognizing and naming internal experiences, staying close to direct perception with phrases like "I feel…," "I smell…," "I think…," or "I do…."

2. Incorporate perspective-taking in your sessions by guiding clients to become aware that their perception is always anchored in their "I," "here," and "now," and that every other person has their own viewpoint of "I-here-now." You can practice multiple different perspectives with them, for example:

   "I-here-now" observing "I-there-now"

   "I" remembering what "I-there-then" experienced

   "I" seeing "you-there-now"

   "I" imagining what "you-there-then" might have felt

   "We" looking together into the same direction

   "I" noticing you, noticing me, noticing you…

3. Support the development of broader, more hierarchical perspectives, including self-compassion, compassion for others, nonjudgmental observation, and values that guide committed actions. Help clients flexibly connect with or gain distance from their experiences; create space for any experience from a broader observer perspective; and guide them in recognizing that they are more than all of their experiences.

Practicing self-as-context with clients often involves something that may initially seem paradoxical: creating distance from thoughts, feelings, and bodily sensations so clients are not consumed by them—while simultaneously embracing these experiences as valid and integral parts of themselves.

It also means being able to take others' perspectives while staying grounded in one's own.

I've come to see self-as-context as multifaceted. Accessing it is different for everyone. It can be a distant perspective or a hierarchical one. It can be a way of observing the flow of events. It can be a safe space—offered by oneself, by another person, or even by something else, like a forest, a lake, or an animal. It can also be a spiritual experience, such as a sense of deep connection, inner freedom, or giving space to the universe.

Self-as-context can be even more, depending on what perspective a person can access in a given moment—and what serves them best.

I see this book as part of a broader cultural evolution—one that will continue to unfold in all areas of life. I wholeheartedly hope the tools offered here can contribute to greater flexibility, well-being, and shared solutions that serve the greater good.

It was heartening to receive this message from Anna, thirteen years old, after a conversation in which we practiced some of these tools:

"Hi Beate, I wanted to thank you so much for your trick with the things you feel and so on. I was just able to help my best friend, and it basically prevented the worst from happening."

We likely still have only a nascent understanding of self-as-context—within or beyond the dimensions of time and space. I am curious to see where future human experience will lead us.

Before I wrap up, I want to acknowledge something: writing this book doesn't make me a master of self-as-context. Even after completing the final chapters, I had moments of doubt—wondering, "Wait… what exactly is self-as-context again?"—and feeling a wave of panic that I'd misunderstood something, said it wrong, or might be judged or misinterpreted.

The only way I could keep writing was by using the very same tools I describe within. I practiced noticing the knot in my stomach, the anxious thoughts telling me I wasn't the right person to write this book, and the imagined critiques. Rather than getting caught up in them, I kept returning to my intention—to contribute something valuable. And I reminded myself that once it's out in the world, how it lands is no longer in my control.

The process taught me many precious lessons I'll carry with me.

Now, it's in your hands.

> You help me find words for what I couldn't express. Now, I can see the beauty I hadn't seen before.
>
> —Peppe, fifty-one years old, construction worker, after a suicide attempt

Acknowledgments

Thanks to my beloved husband Alexander, my sunshine and favorite other-as-context.

A huge thanks to David Lorscheid for helping me clarify my ideas and find my voice as a first-time author, for giving the text its flow with his knowledgeable edits, and for being my faithful companion on this journey.

Thanks to Matthew McKay from New Harbinger, who thought I could write this book, and to his colleagues Elizabeth Hollis Hansen and Madison Davis for their steady encouragement and support.

I'm also grateful to copyeditor MC Calvi for their thoughtful and meticulous final edits.

Thanks to everyone who spent their precious time reading one or more chapters and offering invaluable advice, thought-provoking questions, and stimulating discussions: Ralf Steinkopff, Corinna Stewart, Rainer Sonntag, Tina Käshammer, Noelle Opsahl, Steve Hayes, Louise McHugh, Niklas Törneke, Russ Harris, Joseph Ciarocchi, Anne Bert, Ben Spaloss, Ian Stewart, Stefan Wagler, Angelika Ilmberger, Martin Brüne, Jennifer Kemp, Jenna LeJeune, Rosemarie Weichel, and Hani Alsaaidi.

Thanks to all who supported me with confidence or articles: Jaqueline Pistorello, Andrew Gloster, Louise Hayes, Robyn Walser, Susanne Kohts, and Dagmar Bankamp.

Thanks to my long-term mentors and supervisors in ACBS, who gave me a loving space to grow and to bring my vision to life: Steve Hayes, Rainer Sonntag, and Mavis Tsai.

Thanks to the world best coaches from Landmark Worldwide, who listened to my growth and development and the creation of my vision many years ago: Owen Coffey, Helen Gilhooly, Carolyn Fine, and Helga Christian.

Thanks for the inspiring spiritual knowledge of the ancient Sweet Medicine SunDance Path, shared by Sabina Tschudi and Johannes Schröder.

Thanks to my Commit and Act network all over the world, www.commitandact.org, with whom I learned so much about the bright and the dark sides of human beings, and to Hannah Keittel Vonjoe, my master for intercultural learning and respect.

References

Beebe, B., Cohen, P., & Lachmann, F. (2019). *Bindung im Werden: Mikroanalyse der Mutter-Kind-Interaktion*. Psychosozial-Verlag.

Brach, T. (2013). *Finding true refuge*. Audio DVD. Sounds True.

Ciarrochi, J., Hayes, S. C., Hofmann, S. G., & Sahdra, B. K. (2021). *Assessing processes of change in psychological interventions: The process-based assessment tool (PBAT)*.

Ciarrochi, J., Sahdra, B., Hofmann, S. G., & Hayes, S. C. (2022). Developing an item pool to assess processes of change in psychological interventions: The process-based assessment tool (PBAT). *Journal of Contextual Behavioral Science, 23*, 200–213.

Ciarrochi, J., Hernández, C., Hill, D., Ong, C., Gloster, A. T., Levin, M. E., Yap, K., Fraser, M. I., Sahdra, B. K., Hofmann, S. G., & Hayes, S. C. (2024). Process-based therapy: A common ground for understanding and utilizing therapeutic practices. *Journal of Psychotherapy Integration, 34*(3), 265–290.

Feldman Barrett, L. (2017). *How emotions are made: The secret life of the brain*. Boston: Houghton Mifflin Harcourt.

Flujas-Contreras, J. M., Recio-Berlanga, Á., Andrés, M. P., Fernández-Torres, M., Sánchez-López, P., & Gómez, I. (2023). The relationship between parental stress and psychological adjustment of the children: The role of parental psychological flexibility as a mediator. *Journal of Contextual Behavioral Science, 29*, 202–208.

Fonseca, A., Moreira, H., & Canavarro, M. C. (2020). Uncovering the links between parenting stress and parenting styles: The role of psychological flexibility within parenting and global psychological flexibility. *Journal of Contextual Behavioral Science, 18*, 59–67.

Gloster, A. T., Walder, N., Levin, M. E., Twohig, M. P., & Karekla, M. (2020). The empirical status of acceptance and commitment therapy: A review of meta-analyses. *Journal of Contextual Behavioral Science, 18*, 181–192.

Gloster, A. T., Block, V. J., Klotsche, J., Villanueva, J., Rinner, M. T. B., Benoy, C., Walter, M., Karekla, M., & Bader, K. (2021). Psy-Flex: A contextually sensitive measure of psychological flexibility. *Journal of Contextual Behavioral Science, 22*, 13–23.

Gottman, J. S., & Gottman, J. (2024). *Fight right: How successful couples turn conflict into connection*. New York: Penguin Random House.

Hayes, S. C. (1984). Making sense of spirituality. *Behaviorism, 12*(2), 99–110

Hayes, S. C. (1995). Knowing selves. *The Behavior Therapist, 18*, 94–96.

Hayes, S. C., Strosahl, K. D., & Wilson, K. G. (2004). *Akzeptanz und Commitment Therapie. Ein erlebnisorientierter Ansatz zur Verhaltensänderung.* (Translated by Rainer Sonntag.) CIP-Medien, München.

Hayes, S. C. (2015, June 26). Gay marriage, racism, and obamacare: The challenge of caring. *Psychology Today.* https://www.psychologytoday.com/us/blog/get-out-your-mind/201506/gay-marriage-racism-and-obamacare-the-challenge-caring

Hayes, S. C. (2019). *A liberated mind: How to pivot toward what matters.* New York: Penguin Random House.

Hayes, S. C., Hofmann, S. G., & Wilson D. S. (2020). Clinical psychology is an applied evolutionary science. *Clinical Psychology Review, 81,* 101892.

Hayes, S. C., Law, S., Malady, M., Zhu, Z., Bai, X. (2020). The centrality of sense of self in psychological flexibility processes: What the neurobiological and psychological correlates of psychedelics suggest. *Journal of Contextual Behavioral Science, 15,* 30–38.

Hayes, S. C., Ciarrochi, J., Hofmann, S. G., Chin, F., & Sahdra, B. (2022). Evolving an idionomic approach to processes of change: Towards a unified personalized science of human improvement. *Behaviour Research and Therapy, 156*(7–8), 104155.

Hayes, S. C., & Hofmann, S. G. (2023). A biphasic relational approach to the evolution of human consciousness. *International Journal of Clinical and Health Psychology, 23*(4), 100380.

Hayes, S. C. (2024, June). Email exchange on "Training self-as-context." ACT-trainers listserve.

Hofmann, S. G., Asnaani, A., Vonk, I. J., Sawyer, A. T., & Fang, A. (2012). The efficacy of cognitive behavioral therapy: A review of meta-analyses. *Cognitive Therapy and Research, 36*(5), 427–440.

Hofmann, S. G., Hayes, S. C., & Lorscheid, D. (2021). *Learning process-based therapy.* Oakland, CA: Context Press.

Kuyken, W., and Moulds, M. L. (2009). Remembering as an observer: How is autobiographical memory retrieval vantage perspective linked to depression? *Memory, 17*(6), 624–634.

LeJeune, J., & Luoma, J. B. (2019). *Values in therapy: A clinician's guide to helping clients explore values, increase psychological flexibility, and live a more meaningful life.* Oakland, CA: Context Press.

Luoma, J. B., Sabucedo, P., Eriksson, J., Gates, N., & Pilecki, B. C. (2019). Toward a contextual psychedelic-assisted therapy: Perspectives from acceptance and commitment therapy and contextual behavioral science. *Journal of Contextual Behavioral Science, 14,* 136–145.

Maier, S. F., & Seligman, M. E. P. (2016). Learned helplessness at fifty: Insights from neuroscience. *Psychological Review, 123*(4), 349–367.

Novak, G. (2012). Precursors to perspective-taking. In L. McHugh & I. Stewart (Eds.), *The self and perspective-taking: Contributions and applications from modern behavioral science.* Oakland, CA: Context Press.

McHugh, L., Stewart, I., & Almada, P. (2019). *A contextual behavioral guide to the self: Theory and practice.* Oakland, CA: Context Press.

McHugh, L.,& Stapleton, A. (2021). Self-as-Context. In M. P. Twohig, M. E. Levin, & J. M. Petersen (Eds.), *Oxford handbook of acceptance and commitment therapy.* Oxford Handbooks online.

Ong, C. W., Ciarrochi, J., Hofmann, S. G., Karekla, M., & Hayes, S. C. (2024). Through the extended evolutionary meta-model, and what ACT found there: ACT as a process-based therapy. *Journal of Contextual Behavioral Science, 32,* 100734.

de Saint-Exupéry, A. (1989). *Der kleine Prinz.* München: Wilhelm Heyne Verlag.

Schiraldi, G. R. (2021). *The adverse childhood experiences recovery workbook: Heal the hidden wounds from childhood affecting your adult mental and physical health.* Oakland, CA: New Harbinger Publications.

Schnarch, D. (2011). *Intimität und Verlangen: Sexuelle Leidenschaft wieder wecken.* Stuttgart: Klett-Cotta Verlag.

Skinner, B. F. (1976). *About Behaviorism.* New York: Vintage Books.

Stewart, I., & McHugh, L. (2012). Approaches to the self. In L. McHugh and I. Stewart (Eds.), *The self and perspective-taking. Contributions and applications from modern behavioral science.* Oakland, CA: Context Press.

Strosahl, K., & Robinson, P. (2022). *Focused ACT online course. Module 1, Handbook.* New Harbinger Publications.

Styles, R. G., & Atkins, P. W. B. (2018). Measuring perceptions of self and others in what people say: A replication and extension of the functional self-discrimination measure. *Journal of Contextual Behavioral Science*, 9, 45–52.

Svitak, S. (2021). *Die therapeutische Haltung in ACT: Achtsamkeit in der therapeutischen Beziehung.* Deutschland: Springer-Verlag.

Törneke, N. (2010). *Learning RFT: An introduction to relational frame theory and its clinical applications.* Oakland, CA: Context Press.

Tsai, M., Kohlenberg, R. J., Kanter J. W., Kohlenberg B., Follette W. C., & Callaghan, G. M. (2009). *A guide to functional analytic psychotherapy: Awareness, courage, love, and behaviorism.* New York: Springer.

Villatte, M., Villatte, J., & Hayes, S. C. (2015). *Mastering the clinical conversation: Language as intervention.* New York: Guilford.

Villatte, M. (2024). *Intensive Training on Self as Context.* Online Workshop. https://languageasintervention.com/1290-2/

Walser, R. D., Karlin, B. E., Trockel, M., Mazina, B., & Taylor, C. B. (2013). Training in and implementation of acceptance and commitment therapy for depression in the veterans health administration: Therapist and patient outcomes. *Behaviour Research and Therapy*, 51(9), 555–563.

Wersebe, H., Lieb R., Meyer, A. H., Hoyer, J., Wittchen, H. U., & Gloster, A. T. (2017). Changes of valued behaviors and functioning during an acceptance and commitment therapy intervention. *Journal of Contextual Behavioral Science*, 6(1), 63–70.

Whittingham, Koa (2014). Parenting in context. *Journal of Contextual Behavioral Science*, 3(3), 212–215.

Yu, L., McCracken, L. M., & Norton, S. (2016). The self experiences questionnaire (SEQ): Preliminary analyses for a measure of self in people with chronic pain. *Journal of Contextual Behavioral Science*, 5(3), 127–133.

Zettle, R. D., Gird, S. R., Webster, B. K., Carrasquillo-Richardson, N., Swails, J. A., & Burdsal, C. A. (2018). The self-as-context scale: Development and preliminary psychometric properties. *Journal of Contextual Behavioral Science*, 10, 64–74.

Index

A

B

C

D

E

F

G

H

S

T

U

V

W

Y

Beate M.E. Ebert is a distinguished behavioral clinical psychologist with a private practice in her hometown of Aschaffenburg, Germany. She is a fellow and peer-reviewed acceptance and commitment therapy (ACT) trainer of the Association for Contextual Behavioral Science (ACBS), and a founding member of the German-speaking ACBS Chapter, where she served as a first chairperson. In 2010, she founded Commit and Act Germany (CAA-G), a nonprofit providing psychosocial support in conflict zones such as Sierra Leone in West Africa.

Ebert, along with her team, trained local health workers using methods like ACT and PROSOCIAL, adapted to local culture and challenges. She helped establish Commit and Act Foundation Sierra Leone (CAF-SL), aiding thousands of violence victims and training entire village communities in violence prevention; today it has become one of the most influential non-government organizations in the region. Through her efforts, Ebert also initiated a fruitful communal development partnership between Aschaffenburg, Germany, and Bo, Sierra Leone.

Ebert's contributions were recognized with the Award of Merit from the Bo District Ebola Task Force for her outstanding leadership in fighting the Ebola epidemic in Sierra Leone, Aschaffenburg's Agenda 21 Prize for CAA-G's extraordinary engagement in providing psychosocial support during the Ebola crisis, and the Engagement Prize awarded by the German Federal Ministry for Economic Cooperation and Development for her long-standing, personal, and voluntary commitment to implementing the United Nations' Sustainable Development Goals.

Foreword writer **Steven C. Hayes, PhD**, is Foundation Professor Emeritus at the University of Nevada, Reno; and president of the Institute for Better Health. Author of forty-eight books and more than 700 scientific articles, he has been president of numerous professional organizations and is among the most cited living psychologists. He has shown in his research on relational frame theory (RFT) how and why language and symbolic thought leads both to human achievement and to human suffering, and has guided the extension of RFT to ACT.